To: ADAM

Go Blue
Go Bucks

Jim Falt

Forty Years
in The **BIG**
HOUSE

Forty Years
in The **BIG**
HOUSE

Michigan Tales from
My Four Decades as a Wolverine

Jon Falk with Dan Ewald

TRIUMPH
B O O K S

TRIUMPHBOOKS.COM

Library of Congress Cataloging-in-Publication Data

Falk, Jon, 1949–

Forty years in the big house : Michigan tales from my four decades as a Wolverine / Jon Falk with Dan Ewald.

pages cm

ISBN 978-1-62937-073-6 (hardback)

1. Falk, Jon, 1949– 2. Michigan Wolverines (Football team)—History. 3. University of Michigan—Football—History. I. Ewald, Dan. II. Title.

GV958.U52863F349 2015

796.332'630977435—dc23

2015005863

This book is available in quantity at special discounts for your group or organization. For further information, contact:

Triumph Books LLC
814 North Franklin Street
Chicago, Illinois 60610
(312) 337-0747
www.triumphbooks.com

Printed in U.S.A.
ISBN: 978-1-62937-073-6
Design by Amy Carter
Photos courtesy of Jon Falk unless otherwise indicated

I couldn't be where I am without the love and support of my family.

For my wife, Cheri, and all her support through my career and being my best friend in retirement. To our children, Joe Winkle, Nicki Pfefferle (and husband Kurt), and Katie Falk. To our 16-year-old grandson, Joey Winkle, and our two-year-old granddaughter, Abby Pfefferle. To Cheri's parents, Ramona and Pete Boychuck, who made me a part of their family. And to my mother, Jean Falk, and grandmother, Rosella Land, who encouraged me to follow my dreams.

And a special thanks to Talawanda High School in Oxford, Ohio, for inducting me into the 2012 High School Hall of Fame and Miami University in Oxford, Ohio, for giving me the opportunity to start my career, which would propel my 40-year career at the University of Michigan. Thank you to all the Michigan players, coaches, staff, and fans for all of the wonderful memories to share.

—Jon Falk

I dedicate my 14th and final book to a special group of young and young-at-heart beautiful characters. To my loving wife, Kathy, for all you do for me. To Dan Jr., Amy, Gracie, Andrea, Marc, Isabel, Audrey, Mykell, Kevin, Alex, Todd, Isabel, Leslie, Junior, Paola. I am truly blessed.

—*Dan Ewald*

Contents

Foreword

As a redshirt sophomore at the University of Michigan in 1984, I was preparing to become the starting quarterback the next season. A ruckus broke out between some of my teammates in the dorm where we were housed. The commotion drew some attention. Unfortunately, some of the details slipped down to Bo Schembechler.

Bo was amazing. It seemed like he heard about every little misstep taken by anyone on his team. I can still hear his voice today. "Harbaugh!" he hissed. "You're off the team."

Just like that I was suspended from the team. The experience was somewhat unnerving to say the least.

So as spring break drew closer, it seemed like Big Jon Falk was the only person I could talk to. Big Jon asked if I would like to accompany him on a drive to Miami of Ohio, where he had gone to school and his mother and grandmother lived. Then we drove to Bloomington, Indiana, to visit Jon's great friend Bobby Knight and watch his Indiana team play Michigan.

On the drive home, we shared a lot of thoughts, and Jon suggested that

Following a breakfast to welcome Jim Harbaugh back to the University of Michigan as the football coach, Cheri and Jon Falk stayed to watch the ensuing press conference.

things would work out fine. When we got back from the trip, Big Jon slipped in to see Bo. "I think the young man has learned his lesson," Falk mentioned to Bo. "Don't you think it's time to take him back?"

"Bo brings a player back when he thinks it's the right time," Bo said.

A few days later, Bo brought me back.

I never missed a practice and I learned a lot from both of those men. And a lifelong friendship resulted.

Every football fan realizes and appreciates the responsibilities of all that an equipment manager does. There are the uniforms, helmets, pads, shoes, and all of the random pieces of equipment to handle. But Big Jon takes that commitment to another level. He shares that fervor with every player and coach who has ever taken the field to enhance the tradition of Michigan. The equipment manager is like the spine of the entire team. He holds the team together.

I've seen a lot of good ones, but I've never seen it done better than Jon. He's the best of the best. He's a friend and ally who believes in you. It doesn't matter if you're a raw rookie or an All-American candidate. He treats everyone the same.

No one had a better pulse of the team. He made sure that molehills didn't grow to mountains. I've never seen him rattled. I never saw him make a mistake. The job of an equipment manager is difficult. With 40 years of experience and a well-trained eye, Big Jon made it look easy. That's what the great ones do.

Thanks, Jon, for making life and the University of Michigan just a little bit better for so many friends.

—Jim Harbaugh

Preface

"The essence of Michigan football lies not in the bodies of all those magnificent players who bravely take the field each Saturday in the fall. It lives proudly, rather, in the spirit of all the players, all the coaches, all the students, all the alumni, and all the fans for all the men and women—past, present, and future—who strive for excellence through honesty, integrity, and hard work. That's the Michigan way."

—Bo Schembechler

Hall of Famer Sparky Anderson met Michigan football legend Bo Schembechler soon after becoming the Detroit Tigers manager in 1979. The two believed there are more similarities than differences between coaching the nation's finest athletes, regardless of the sport.

For instance, Sparky and Bo believed that a locker room is the first step toward success. If the locker room is sloppy and undisciplined, the character of that team will eventually slip away. Sparky also maintained that if a writer or a broadcaster really wants to understand the make-up or character of the team, he should look around the locker room and talk to the clubhouse manager.

Nobody spends more time in the locker room than the locker room manager. He knows everything that's going on. "Now that manager must not break any confidences," Anderson said. "That locker room is sacred ground."

Bo trusted Jon Falk as much as he did each captain of his teams. So did Bo's successors—Gary Moeller, Lloyd Carr, Rich Rodriguez, and Brady Hoke. That's a giant size compliment Falk still keeps close to his heart. That's how you spend 40 years in such a place of trust.

—Dan Ewald

Introduction

Forty years at the University of Michigan. It does not feel that long. There are buildings at Michigan that did not last as long as I have. Those buildings that have lasted at least 40 years learned how to withstand the rumbling of gusty winds, the heat of scorching summers, and the ice cold temperatures of winter. They've survived because all of those buildings were built with an unshakable foundation and an equally immovable support structure.

The reason I was able to last 40 years at Michigan was because Michigan provided me with a solid foundation and a great support system. There have been some rough times, but the university has always provided the support we all need.

When I came to Michigan, I was 23 years old and not much older than the players I worked with. Bo taught me about the dedication, desire, and passion that it takes to work and play at Michigan. Bo told me to take that passion into the locker room and make sure the players learn what it takes to win the Big Ten championship.

I remember my first game week at Michigan. I had to come up with an idea to get the players to pack their equipment to move it to the stadium and I wanted to make it fun for the players, too. I came up with a black mesh bag with a laundry pin that had the player's jersey number on it to seal the bag. September 12, 1974, was the first official initial Black Bag Day. I was in the locker room telling the players to pack their black bags so we could move them to Michigan Stadium to play football and represent the University of Michigan.

Black Bag Day became a tradition for all home games.

I was telling the freshmen what to pack and what it will be like dressing at Michigan Stadium. The whole time I was yelling, "Pack your black bags... Michigan Stadium, here we come!"

What a privilege it is to play in Michigan Stadium and run down the Tunnel and play for such a traditional giant of a program. People who watch the players emerge from the Tunnel do not realize how much the players had to persevere to earn their right to be there. I can't run down that tunnel anymore, but I know what it takes to get there—the pride and tradition behind the Tunnel.

People ask what I miss most now. It's the players, being in the locker room before the game, rubbing the players' heads, or patting each player's shoulder pads as he heads for the field. "Play your best for Michigan!" I'd shout to each one.

Watching a player turn a terrifically tough play was always special. Seeing the smiling face of a player who just scored for Michigan was priceless. And hugging the guys after they were done celebrating was well worth the wait.

The great thing about Michigan is its foundation. Because of that foundation, all of these things and a lifetime of traditions will carry on. I just will not be there to see them firsthand. But my heart will always be part of the program.

I will always cherish all of my old sayings, such as "it's black bag day, men" or "pack your travel bags, men, it's get away day" for road trips or after a great win on the road. After singing "The Victors" in the locker room, I'd walk around the room saying: "Let's get outta this hell hole and go home."

All these little things are what used to make autumn Saturdays so very special. Yes, these are the little things that I miss so much, but I am not crying because those days are over. I am smiling because it all happened. And I was blessed to have shared in them. The players, coaches, and staff made each of my days happy memories. Where else could anyone celebrate such a strong foundation or a better support structure?

And I hope every player will remember that his next ring will always be his best ring. I was privileged to help carry the passion and determination to all the players for five football head coaches called Bo, Mo, Carr, RichRod, and Brady Hoke. As Fritz Crisler said: "Tradition is something you can't bottle up…you can't go down and buy it at the corner store…but it is there to sustain you when you need it most. I have watched countless Michigan athletes and countless Michigan coaches call upon it time and time again. There is nothing like it…I hope it never dies."

—Jon Falk

Chapter 1
Life with Bo

Soon after Jon Falk moved to Ann Arbor, he spent a lot of evening dinners at the Schembechler residence. At the time, Falk was living in a postage-stamp-size-second-floor apartment located in the clubhouse of the university golf course. He could lean his back up against one wall and stretch his legs up against the opposite wall.

Bo's wife, Millie, never did see the inside of that apartment, but she did sense that Falk was lonesome from worrying about his mother and grandmother back in Oxford, Ohio. So Millie tried to make Falk, a man in his early 20s, feel more comfortable and at home. Falk enjoyed those meals with the Schembechler family, which included fine cooking and good conversation. It also offered Bo and Jon the opportunity to establish a friendship that stretched far beyond the football field.

One evening after dinner, Millie, Bo, the kids, and Falk were sitting around the table when a question from Millie silenced all of the small talk. "Sometimes you appear to be somewhat fearful of Bo," she innocently inquired. "Is that the case?"

Falk took a half-glass gulp of water and quickly looked at the faces around the table. The boys were giggling. Bo got that glaze of curiosity in his eyes. And Millie simply smiled politely.

"I'm not exactly sure about what you mean by fearful of Bo," Falk began carefully. "But I sure do respect him an awful lot."

Everybody around the table broke into a relieved laugh, and Falk felt he had been accepted into the family in a most peculiar way. "You really had to stay close to Bo to understand all the nuances of his strength and commitment to his teams," Falk said. "He also had that commitment to the University of Michigan and all the friends he made along the way. I was fortunate to have gotten so close to him. It was a lifelong learning process. So many laughs and lessons to be learned along the way."

Bo would have remained coaching Michigan, but his cardiologist friend, Dr. Kim Eagle, recommended his stepping away from the stress of coaching after the Rose Bowl game of January 1990. Even Falk was shocked at that news. A few days later, Bo dropped another bomb that shook the foundation of college football and Major League Baseball at the same time.

Bo was going to become a Detroit Tiger.

Not as the manager. Not even as a coach.

Falk got one of the heartiest laughs on his best buddy after Bo returned from his press conference at Tiger Stadium to announce he had been named president of the Detroit Tigers. Implausible as such a notion like that sounded, Bo confirmed it was true. After a short visit to his office, Bo went to the football locker room for a workout designed to help him relax and to help his heart become healthier.

After opening his locker, Bo felt a shock even bigger than the announcement. He immediately shouted for Falk. Emerging from a corner, Falk walked up to Bo.

"What's the matter here, Bo?" Falk had to fight to keep from laughing.

"Where's my workout stuff?" Bo barked at Falk. "My shoes. My shirt. My shorts. All my stuff. My whole damn locker is empty."

Members of the coaching staff had to fight off their own laughter while hiding in corners of the room. "Well, Bo," Falk struggled to remain straight, "they told me you were no longer with the University of Michigan. They say you're a Detroit Tiger now."

It had become customary that when an assistant coach or member of the staff retired or moved to another job, Bo would call Falk and inform him to clean out the departing person's locker. "Falk," Bo would bark into the phone, "[so and so] is leaving. Clean out the locker. He's gone. He's not working for the University of Michigan anymore."

"Well, they come and they go, Hobbs," Falk would relay to Bo when the locker was empty. "They come and they go."

That classic line is from the baseball novel *The Natural* written by the celebrated Bernard Malamud and made into a movie starring Robert Redford as Roy Hobbs.

This time, the surprise was on Bo.

Falk let his friend stew for a moment. "Well," Falk finally drawled. "You know what happens around here. They come and they go, Hobbs…they come and they go."

Falk finally broke into a laugh. So did all the assistant coaches and team staff members, who crawled out from behind their hiding corners.

The bond between Bo and Falk became even stronger after the Tigers were sold, and Bo was relieved of his duties. After Millie died, Bo married Cathy, and the couple became world travelers. Of course, all trips were put on hold until after the football season. Bo entrusted Falk to take care of the Schembechler home while the couple was away. But the ol' coach made sure never to impinge upon Falk's principal responsibilities to the football program.

Falk already was well-entrenched in his primary job, so there was no conflict with helping his friend. "I never really thought of our relationship as best friends," Falk reflected about Bo. "My gig was to work and do things for the head football coach. No matter who that was, I always felt proud about the fact that every coach at Michigan could depend on me. I liked that. I liked the confidence of dependability. That's one of the things I miss most. I miss it because that was my identity. Someone used to call on me when there was a problem they couldn't fix themselves. That's the part I miss. Bo probably put more pressure on me because he knew I could get the problem taken care of quickly. I enjoyed that feeling. It was a lifetime learning process for me, and no one in the country had a better time than I did."

Falk admits he probably underestimated how much Bo came to rely on him to fix an assortment of little problems. "You have to remember that no matter how good a friend is, there still is an employer/employee relationship that must be upheld," Falk said. "There were times when Bo would have me go to his house or go on a short trip with him. But he always made sure I tended to my team responsibilities first."

The first consideration was always the team.

From Falk's first day on the job in February 1974 and throughout the years, Bo always reminded Falk that the most important role he had was to "help the Michigan team to win the Little Brown Jug, the Paul Bunyan Trophy, and above all the Big Ten championships."

After 40 years in that same position, coaches, staffs, players, and fans in every city of the Big Ten and the bowl games came to recognize the most experienced man in his position. "I was so fortunate to have the best school and best teams anywhere in the country," Falk told Bo about a week before the coach's death. "I thank you for the opportunity you gave me."

Bo eyed his friend with a peaceful look—one that suggested their friendship would be eternal. "Nothing truly good is ever just given to anyone," Bo said. "You made the position better than it was when you started. That honor belongs to you. No one else can claim that. You've come a long way from Oxford, Ohio. You're going be remembered around here for a long time."

One of the most satisfying visits that Bo made was to meet with General Norman Schwarzkopf when the celebrated warrior and commander of Desert Storm was in Detroit. The general and Bo had a terrific time swapping stories about the direction of the country and which political party is better suited to make the necessary fixes to ensure peace and prosperity throughout the country. General H. Norman Schwarzkopf was admired by Bo. One of Bo's favorite quotes from the general was: "I admire men of character and I judge character not by how a man deals with his superiors, but mostly how he deals with his subordinates. That is where you find out what the character of a man is." Bo was just like that. He treated all of his subordinates with great respect.

It should not be surprising that Bo's and Jon's political convictions happen to coincide so closely with the general's. Bo was invited, along with the entire 1997 National Championship football team, to the White House in April of 1998. However, being the staunch Republican he was, he politely refused. Bo never compromised his convictions regardless of the title in front of someone's title or name. A couple of months after Bo died, President Clinton spoke at the university's commencement held in The Big House. "I'd also like to acknowledge I'm here in the football stadium which I have watched on television a hundred times, that this is the first graduation to occur after the passing of Bo Schembechler, who, as most of you know, was quite an ardent Republican," Bill Clinton said. "As I walked in here today on university soil, I considered a philosophical question that I had never before

Honored for winning the 1997 National Championship, the Michigan team gathers at the White House.

considered, which is whether it is possible still to switch parties in the after-life and whether it would be moral to pray for such a result."

Of course, all the people on the field and all of the parents and relatives of the graduates laughed appropriately at Clinton's remarks. But despite their political and philosophical differences, Falk is quite certain the president and Bo would have had an enjoyable evening trading stories from their lives' experiences. Clinton also took the time to relay to the students how proud he was to walk down that tunnel where so many success stories—including President Ford's time as a student and player—began in The Big House.

Falk came to realize that as much as he felt fulfilled by being able to help people out of any kind of jam, Bo might have felt even more fulfilled helping those who needed it. When it finally struck Bo that he could extend that help to more people in retirement, he accepted that opportunity. "He became more relaxed and didn't feel any pressure," Falk said. "Just like I did, Bo truly enjoyed helping other people. He had the power to pick up a phone and pretty much get done whatever he thought was the right thing to do."

For instance, the list of celebrities for Bo's first charity golf tournament during his first year of retirement fell a couple of players short a few days before the event. Not a problem for Bo. He placed one phone call to baseball legend Pete Rose. He placed another to Yogi Berra. With two quick calls, the roster was complete. "Now that's filling an All-Star roster, Falk," he joked with his friend.

Falk was deeply moved by one of Bo's observations on retirement. "The thing that Bo always said was, 'Nobody got me,'" Falk said. "'Nobody fired me. Nobody had to tell me when to get out. I did it myself. I did it my way.'"

Falk knew how critical it was to Bo to leave Michigan in better shape than when he arrived. "Bo didn't have to worry about the condition of the program he was turning over to Gary Moeller and his staff," Falk said. "He restored the relevance of Michigan football and set the table for decades to come."

He also was instrumental helping to get Michigan players into the College Football Hall of Fame. He made sure the voters knew what type of

When Bo Schembechler held his charity golf tournament, Big Jon arranged a visit from Pete Rose, the all-time leader in major league hits.

When Hall of Fame legend Sparky Anderson managed the Detroit Tigers, Big Jon visited him at the ballpark a couple of times each summer.

man a Michigan Man really is. And Falk is grateful for the many friendships he developed from his long relationship with Bo even after Bo left Michigan to serve as Tigers president. "It's impossible not to like Big Jon," said long-time Tigers shortstop Alan Trammell. "He treats everyone like he's known them all their lives. I'm a sports junkie just like Jon, and it's fun to get his take on anything that happens in the world of sports. He's a good man, always ready to lend a hand."

Falk's favorite baseball friend was Hall of Fame manager Sparky Anderson. Sparky was ill the summer before he died in November of 2010. Nevertheless, he willed his way to visit his friends in Ann Arbor in July. "I remember the look on RichRod's face when he looked up from his desk and saw Sparky staring at him," Falk said. "Sparky made Rich feel like he had come there just to see him. That's the kind of guy Sparky was. Actually, I think Sparky was not feeling well and wanted to visit as many friends as he could. He wanted to reminisce that day, and we spent a lot of time talkin' about the Tigers and his Cincinnati Reds teams. I miss Bo and Sparky every day."

When Tommy Amaker coached Michigan basketball before moving to Harvard, Falk and Amaker developed a personal relationship. "Tommy called one day and asked me to visit his office," Falk said. "He said he had been checking around about me and received a lot of the same compliments from several sources. They said I was honest and upfront. That's what any coach in any sport needs to be successful. Bobby Knight said the same thing. And so did Tom Izzo."

Knight, the legendary Indiana basketball coach, was asked by the University of Michigan to deliver a eulogy to Bo on the field in The Big House immediately before Bo's burial. Knight agreed, but only if Michigan promised to have Falk read it.

Chapter 2

Bo's Boy

Sometime during Bo Schembechler's 21-year coaching career at the University of Michigan and Jon Falk's 40-year marathon stint as Michigan football equipment manager, Falk was teasing Bo in his office. One day Bo needed a dollar for the vending machine. Falk was walking by, so Bo asked Jon if he had a dollar to buy a Coke. When Falk pulled out his billfold, Bo noticed a lottery ticket. "What the hell do you have that for?" Bo asked. "We pay you well, and you will never find a better job than this one."

Falk replied, "Coach, the minute my ticket hits, I'm walking straight into your office and I'm going to tell you, 'Jon Falk is out of here.'" Bo started at Falk and then finally started to grin, "Boy, Jon, before you do all of that, you better make sure you have all six numbers."

The two friends laughed. They were sparring partners and loved to tease each other. Bo knew his loyal friend would never leave the University of Michigan even if he did hit the jackpot. The university was his home. The football program was his life.

Finally after 40 years in the job Falk treasured even more than a giant pizza and a couple of cold Diet Cokes on a Saturday night after a victory, he stepped down after the 2013 season. But even in his well-earned retirement, Falk still is regarded as being one of "Bo's Boys." He's proud of that distinction and all of the things he learned about football and life from Bo. For Falk, being one of Bo's Boys is a legitimate badge of honor.

Falk was just 23 years old when he was personally recruited by Bo out of Miami of Ohio, where Bo had been the head coach, and Falk was still an assistant equipment manager. Bo was a master recruiter. Always was. What and who he really wanted, he usually wound up getting. Not just a train load of offensive players blessed with brute finesse. And not merely a collection of speedy mayhem makers for his always destructive defense.

Bo had a gift for mixing a beautiful blend of assistant coaches and football staff members who shared his basic philosophy: "No man is more important than the team." Bo's words will live forever, like "No coach is more important than the team. The team. The team. The team." Bo spotted that gift of loyalty in Falk and wasn't going to lose him. Bo was always good at spotting potential and then cherry picking the best.

Bo liked the way Falk was organized in the distribution of uniforms and equipment to the team. He also liked Falk's knack for keeping order and just the right balance of humor and calm in the locker room. He saw how Falk anticipated any potential problems. And if one began to fester, Falk possessed the ingenuity to fix it before it sped out of control.

Falk was reliable. Honest. Trustworthy. Above all else he was more loyal than a priceless, hand-crafted Swiss clock. He knew when a secret had to be kept between the head coach and himself. He knew when it was time to say a few words to lift a player at just the right time. He instilled a sense of confidence that made players feel prepared, confident, and comfortable—on the field and in the locker room.

So when needing a head equipment manager at Michigan, Bo hand-picked Falk to join him with the Wolverines in 1974. It wasn't easy finalizing the deal. And it had nothing to do with a salary impasse. It was, in fact, a sensitive situation that challenged Bo to harness all of his recruiting talents—and a few he kept deep in his pockets for sticky and stubborn situations such as this—to get the job done.

Falk originally turned down the offer to join Michigan. Certainly not because he had any reservations about the university or the master coach himself. It was rather that Falk felt compelled to remain in Oxford, Ohio, to better care for the two ladies of his life.

That's when Bo turned his target to Mama Jean Falk and Grandma Rosella Land to win this particular recruiting battle that wound up paying dividends to the university for the next 40 years. Bo convinced Mama Falk and Grandma Land that an offer to work for the University of Michigan is a once-in-a-lifetime opportunity. Such an opportunity would, in fact, even better serve the two ladies in Falk's life. And the drive between Oxford, Ohio, and Ann Arbor is only a couple of hours long on the convenient I-75 highway.

The two ladies—as Bo had planned—did the rest. "You've got to make the move," Mama Falk assured her son. "The University of Michigan and Coach Schembechler will take good care of you."

And while Bo was convinced Falk made the best fit for what he considered to be a critical position on the team staff, even he never could have imagined Falk's 40 years of storybook loyalty. "Loyalty was the easy part," Falk chuckled. "Why would anyone want to go to any university other than Michigan? And who in his right mind would ever choose to leave? Working for Bo and all of the coaches was more of a privilege than a job."

But 40 years? It seems like a real time warp.

That's more than two lifetimes in today's volatile, mega-million dollar world of professional and major college sports where personnel changes often explode like corn kernels in a red hot popper. Falk, however, raised loyalty to another level. Early in his career, Falk heard the whispers about how some of the personnel felt they had to be careful with what they said around Bo's Boy.

But Falk quickly erased any suspicions about his dedication and loyalty to the team with his professional performance that surpassed even the expectations of Bo himself. "It started with Bo and it continued with each coach I served," Falk said. "When the head coach needs something you get it done—immediately. Not just in a few moments, but right now! That's why a good equipment manager has to anticipate every possible situation. There's no better feeling in my job than having a coach tell me to do something and I can say to him it's already been done."

During the last 40 years, whenever a sticky problem occurred in the locker room or on the field, Falk was usually called upon to fix it. And even though it might have been a makeshift solution, it did the job until a more permanent resolution could be devised. It could have been a faulty phone line from the field to the press box where the assistants worked the game. Falk fixed the problem. Or it could have been that one of the assistant coaches needed help starting his car after a game. Falk at least got the car started…or got someone there quickly to take the car to the repair shop. "You're not just an equipment manager anymore," one of the university officials chuckled. "You're an expediter."

An old inter-office memorandum demonstrating the versatility of Falk was retrieved from a file belonging to former Michigan athletic director Don Canham. It refers to an incident that occurred before the November 19, 1983, game against Ohio State and was delivered to appropriate athletic staff officials. It reads:

> I thought we had a manual as to what would be done at the Michigan Stadium each game. One incident occurred that indicates the left hand doesn't know what the right hand is doing.
>
> When we took the tarpaulin off the field prior to the game, the area around the Tunnel and beyond the hash mark was deep in water. I looked around for someone to find out where the squeegees were and who was assigned

to squeegee the field and could find no one. That should have been our first priority. We all know that we had to have a dry field to play on. I finally ended up going to Jon Falk who had far more on his mind than squeegee-ing the field. He grabbed some young people out of the stands, located the squeegees, and squeegeed the field prior to the teams coming on the field.

In the future, I want a rainy day plan with 100 men armed with 100 squeegees assigned to man the squeegees. There was a corner of the end zone that never did get squeegeed, but I didn't see it until I got in the press box.

We have been through this many times, and the only way to get the water off the field is with squeegees.

I do not want this to happen again in the future.

—Don Canham

The message to a variety of department heads was anything but subtle. Don Canham does not conduct himself in a way that anyone would consider subtle. "When you gotta squeegee, you gotta squeegee," Falk simply smiled. "The main thing is to get the job done. That's always the case whatever the problem is. Get the job done."

To gain perspective on Falk's tenure at Michigan, when he first arrived in Ann Arbor in 1974, computers were still in their infancy. Some of the early models were the size of an entire room. The price of gas did not swallow away half a month's paycheck. Telephone booths still speckled the corners on many streets in most major cities. And who would have thought that eventually a phone would fit into a shirt's tiniest pocket?

Schembechler Hall was only a glint in the back of the university's imagination. And so were a handful of academic buildings that continued to spring up throughout the campus. The war in Vietnam was inching closer toward its nebulous end. The infamous Watergate scandal, however, was racing toward its inglorious finish.

It was the year Al Kaline was finishing his Hall of Fame playing career with the Detroit Tigers. Billy Martin was one year removed from his three-year stint as manager of the Tigers. Joe Schmidt was two years removed from coaching the Detroit Lions. Four-year starting quarterback Rick Leach was one year away from playing his first game as a true freshman quarterback for the Wolverines. And Bo had yet to notch his first victory in the Horseshoe at Ohio State. In politics, just east down the I-94 Freeway from Ann Arbor, Coleman Young was in the middle of his first term during his 20-year run as Detroit's first African American mayor.

With Falk's retirement after the 2013 season, the string of Bo's Boys came to an end. "Forty years!" Falk shook his head in disbelief. "I can't explain it. But it sure goes to show how working at a school like Michigan truly does make time fly."

Faster, in fact, than a downfield Tom Brady touchdown pass. "Working with the coaches and players I was privileged to have served made all the difference in the world," Falk said. "There's only one University of Michigan."

And now a year after retirement from having established himself as one of the most accomplished and colorful characters in the game, Falk enjoys reminiscing about all the good times and challenges that were part of his daily menu. He still enjoys that late summer tingle when news of college football begins to challenge Major League Baseball for space in the newspapers and air time on the radio and television.

He relishes those special phone calls and visits from former Michigan players scattered around the country. Most call simply to see how Big Jon is doing. He loves those opportunities of talking to former Michigan coaches such as Gary Moeller, Lloyd Carr, Jerry Hanlon, and Tirrell Burton, who still reside in the Ann Arbor area.

And he remains forever grateful for simply talking to Michigan football fanatics who still stop him on the street just to share a few moments of his time and memories from the "good old days." Not only does Falk entertain

Son-in-law Kurt Pfefferle, daughter Nicki Pfefferle, granddaughter Abby Pfefferle, wife Cheri Falk, Jon Falk, daughter Katie Falk, grandson Joey Winkle, and son Joe Winkle commemorate Jon's 40 years at Michigan.

them with his pinpoint descriptions of any games of their choice, he does so with total recall of every key play.

Some of those plays will live forever in the memories of the world-wide Michigan faithful. Since 1969, only six men are privileged to have served the University of Michigan as head football coach. Jim Harbaugh checks in at No. 6. The first five are: Bo, Moeller, Carr, Rich Rodriguez, and Brady Hoke. Falk is the only member of the football staff to have served the first five. Falk also is the only football staff member to have served the last seven athletic directors. They include the legendary Canham, Bo, Jack Weidenbach, Joe Roberson, Tom Goss, Bill Martin, and Dave Brandon.

Falk is truly a walking, talking history book about Michigan football. And despite that matter of his retirement, he remains on call to lend his expertise to Coach Harbaugh or someone in the athletic department needing his experience and assistance. Falk still is "Bo's Boy." And will forever be.

Chapter 3
A Material Man

Thirty years before Falk was born in 1949, University of Michigan legend Fielding H. Yost defined the role of the ideal Michigan football equipment manager. Yost never did get the opportunity to work with his imagined model. It just took a little time for all the pieces to coalesce. And with his gift for precise details that the legend gave to all of his projects, no one could have done it better.

Coupled with Falk's unshakable loyalty throughout his 40-year run that ended after the 2013 season, Falk completed his career with a performance that would have made Yost feel proud. As the most successful football coach of his era, Yost appreciated any professional who bled as tirelessly into his job as much as he did to his. It didn't matter if it was a job on the field or one behind the scenes. All that mattered was what it meant to the team.

Yost would have felt more than satisfied with the way Falk fit the legend's blueprint. As a visionary, Yost would have been proud of the way Falk enhanced a position into more meaning than it had when Falk took the job. It's a position that affects every individual in the program from coaches and players to the sweepers of the locker room long after a mud-filled practice field.

Yost's footprints remain an indelible part of the campus in the sports complex of his vision. As head football coach (1901–23 and 1925–26), Yost's teams posted a 165–29–10 record. His first team outscored the opposition 550–0 for the season. That included a 49–0 clobbering of Stanford in the inaugural Rose Bowl on January 1, 1902.

From 1901 through 1904, Michigan did not lose a game and was tied only once. That was the game against Minnesota that led to the creation of the Little Brown Jug tradition, college football's oldest trophy game. Yost's teams won six national football championships and 10 Big Ten titles. He also served as athletic director from 1921 through 1940. It was in that role where Yost left his biggest footprint on the entire Michigan athletic program. That enormous achievement still sets the standard for college athletics.

Under his leadership The Big House, Yost Fieldhouse, and the university's golf course were constructed, along with the first on-campus building dedicated solely to intramural sports. Beyond any measure, his 40 years of dreams and promises kept before stepping down after three years (1941–43) of reduced service as athletic director emeritus comprise the most glory-filled period of any Michigan Man in history.

Yost was more than a mere dreamer. He was a visionary, a genius immeasurably ahead of his time. That vision is captured in a pair of letters dated December 13, 1919 and December 16, 1919. Both letters were directed to Phil G. Bartelme, who was the presiding athletic director to whom Yost reported. Both letters are preserved in Michigan's Bentley Library.

In his December 13 letter, Yost writes:

> I think there should be a "material man" to look
> after the football material and its distribution, etc. That
> was quite a source of friction this year. There is a grow-
> ing tendency to complain of many little things that
> were never even considered not long ago. However, this

Jon Falk explains the history of the Little Brown Jug, a tradition started during the Fielding Yost era, to ESPN's Holly Rowe.

situation must be met and everything done to keep up
the spirit and morale of the squad possible.

The second letter, written just three days later, is almost a singular plea
for the hiring of what Yost terms a "property man."

Yost writes:

There should be a property man in charge of the
distribution of all equipment, looking after cleaning the
shoes, repair work, etc. The shoes are not generally
cleated and returned until after the boys are dressed
Saturday for the game. We need much more light for
after dark practice. What we have is too dim, and there
should be someone in charge to see that these lights are
turned on and off at the proper time during the practice
season.

The practice field should be marked off more fre-
quently so that the lines are always plain and distinct
for practice work.

Someone should look after proper horns and whistles, stopwatches for the officials of the game, and to
see that officials have those at each game and get them
afterward. The 10 yards chain we have does not seem
to be the right length, and the head linesmen have been
kicking and adjusting it this fall. This chain should be
measured and if not the exact length, have it made
so. Someone should be in charge and have the proper
whistles, horns, chains, etc. ready for scrimmage each
evening. The boys in charge of the balls are too small
and do not look after them well enough, and one usually
has to send to the clubhouse for the white ball, etc.

It should be someone's duty to look after the admis-
sion of visiting teams, delivery of their trunks, meeting
them at trains, etc.

Quite a litany of responsibilities for one man. But to maintain Michigan as the envy of every football team in America, these and other concerns demanded immediate attention. As athletic director in 1921, Yost got his man when he hired Henry Hatch as football equipment manager, and Hatch held the position for 43 years.

Hatch was a tireless worker and completely committed to the success of the program. By the time he retired, however, college football was in its early stage of revolutionary change. The sport was generating more interest with lightning speed. College football was expanding at the rate of suburbs springing up around major cities throughout the country. The job of equipment manager called for younger hands, feet, and eyes. And above all else a basket full of fresh ideas.

The game was going big time. And to dominate that big-time level, all the pieces had to fit snugly. No longer were conferences and out-of-conference rivalries restricted by regional boundaries. Media coverage exploded with atomic force. Radio broadcasts expanded to the most remote regions of almost every state. Spirited cross-country rivalries became the menu of Saturday afternoon television specials. Multiple writers and columnists from the nation's leading newspapers and magazines were assigned to marquee games to help neutralize the power of the electronic media. By the mid-70s, the role and responsibilities of the equipment manager kept rising wildly at the speed of today's national debt.

Of course, the issuance and maintenance of uniforms and equipment remained the primary duties of the equipment manager as Yost had long ago depicted. Now, however, there were telephone lines between the head coach on the field and assistant coaches in the press box that this material man had to install and maintain. New lines of shoes and other items of equipment had to be secured and maintained. Trucks to road games carrying a houseful of equipment, uniforms, and medical supplies needed to be secured. Assistance and direction for television and radio lines became a pregame necessity.

And once a game was over, everything had to be cleaned and securely stored in its proper place for practice come Monday. Quite a work load. But the Wolverines were fortunate. They had Jon Falk, the man who provided color into an otherwise dull background of dirty gray sweatshirts and muddy cleats.

A hulking figure at 6'3" and 273 pounds and coupled with a belly laugh that could make Santa Claus envious, Falk enjoyed befriending all members of the national and local media by spinning yarns about his beloved Wolverines with the engaging charm of Will Rogers. His tireless interaction with the media helped enhance the romance of Michigan football. "Jon is a character," said the late Michigan All-American and All-Pro tight end Ron Kramer. "He makes people laugh, makes 'em feel good. Nothing wrong with that. He makes the media want to cover Michigan. He was just the right guy to come along in history at the time that he did. Jon's got more phone numbers of former players and coaches and media members around the country than a New York talent agency. And not just those in football. I always said Jon Falk is the rock star of equipment managers. You won't find anyone better. And you always walk away with a smile from Big Jon. No one does a job better than him. And with Jon, Michigan always comes first."

Coming from a character such as Kramer himself, that's quite a compliment that few can equal. "It was always easy for me to talk about Michigan," Falk explained. "Still is. We have more wins than any school in history, and stories about all the great players can fill a whole library. There's magic to all those football games that played on the big stage of The Big House."

Chapter **4**

"The Indispensable Man"

anging in high school and college sports locker rooms across the
country is a 1959 poem written by Saxon White Kessinger. Even
though the celebrated Idaho poet may not have attended a football game in
her life, her poem, titled "The Indispensable Man," captures the essence of
team sports and the unified teamwork demanded of champions.

It reads:

> *Sometimes when you're feeling important;*
> *Sometimes when your ego's in bloom;*
> *Sometimes when you think that you are*
> *The best qualified man in the room;*
> *Sometimes when you think that your absence*
> *would leave an unfillable hole;*
> *Just follow these simple instructions*
> *And see how they humble your soul.*

Take a bucket and fill it with water;
Put your hand in it up to your wrist;
Then take it back out and the hole that remains;
Is the measure of how much you'll be missed.
Now you can splash as much as you want to
You can stir up the water for sure;
Then stop and you see in a moment,
That the water's the same as before.

Now the moral to this is quite simple;
You must do the best that you can,
But you'll always be wise to remember:
There is no indispensable man.

Falk never did hang a copy of the poem on any locker room wall. But he remains rabidly touched by the spirit of its message. More than memorizing the poem word for word, he preached and practiced its essence daily throughout the season as he spread the spirit that no team can reach its potential without the strength of each man sitting to the right or left of every person privileged to be sitting in the locker room.

After arriving at the University of Michigan, Jon Falk understood fully and quickly that every coach, player, and staff member was expected to embrace Bo's concept of "the team…the team…the team."

There is no indispensable man. And no one better think he's any sort of exception. In turn Bo made it emphatically clear that each individual recruited to serve Michigan must be prepared to accept the trust each member has invested in those who were chosen. And that also included all coaching and staff members.

Nothing meant more to Bo than "the team." Bo believed in that indescribable sense of camaraderie and commitment. And it all began in the locker room. Bo demanded that each player on each one of his teams to be united with all of his players before taking that first step onto the practice field. Consequently, Falk embraced the concept of the team as much as his healthy and respectful disdain for the Ohio State Buckeyes.

The locker room of any professional or major college sports team is one of the most sacred parcels of square footage anywhere in any stadium. Some locker rooms are as spacious as a parking lot and auspicious enough to feature video games. And some are so inauspicious that players have to run around in the shower room just to get wet. "I can't explain the mystique of the locker room, but I know it's there," Falk said. "It's easier to feel than to explain."

What's most important about the locker room are the bonds and trust that take shape in one of those members-only refuges where game plans and attitudes are created and perfected. And then they are shared for life. Of even more importance are the memories and lifelong friendships that can only be created in this modest arena primarily limited to coaches, players, team staff members, officials, and—at appointed times—a restricted amount of accredited members of the media.

In no other place than the locker room can the trust and loyalty of a diverse collection of individuals bond so permanently. It's in that locker room where boys grow into men. And sometimes during times of triumph, men are allowed to momentarily slip back into that period of time when all felt young. "Because this group of guys spend every day together—good or bad—there's a special sense of camaraderie that can't be found anywhere else," Falk explained. "It's hard to explain. It's more of a feeling than anything concrete. A man should be able to lay a $100 bill in his locker and know for a fact that it will be there in the same place when practice is over. That's a special kind of feeling for a special kind of a young man."

When Falk was hired as equipment manager, Bo emphasized that Falk's primary responsibility was management of the locker room. Maintaining the distribution of all uniforms and equipment is a painstaking job. But maintaining the spirit and integrity of the locker room became his primary responsibility. "I can still hear Bo's voice today," Falk said with a smile. "'Your No. 1 job is to do everything possible to help this team win the Little Brown Jug, the Paul Bunyan Trophy, and, above all, Big Ten championships, whatever it takes. And that begins right here in the middle of the locker room.'"

"Whatever it takes"—that's how Falk addressed each day, and that mantra wound up being part of 17 Big Ten championship teams. "One of the highest compliments I ever received came from Coach Lloyd Carr," Falk recalled. "He called me the locker room coach because I had the trust of all those young men. I made sure to be one of the first men in the locker room each morning and one of the last to leave at night."

Along with his regular responsibilities, Falk used that time to teach players that after a painful loss, redemption was only one week away. And after a particularly sweet victory, true winners appreciate that celebration is only for the moment. There are two distinct locker rooms used by the Michigan team. One is for gameday at the stadium, which coaches and players share. The other is at Schembechler Hall, where coaches and players are separated during the week.

Because of Falk's various responsibilities to both coaches and players, he had to bounce freely through both, and a fine line of trust had to be established between the players and himself. Falk always found time to lend a shoulder to a struggling player and was painfully careful to walk that tightrope of trust between coach and player. "If a particular player felt disgruntled about something, I made it my job to talk to the player," Falk said. "There were times I discreetly had to share some information with the coach about a certain problem that might need his attention. A player's trust must always be maintained."

Former longtime assistant coach Jerry Hanlon feels Falk did the best job of maintaining that trust along with making the coach understand that a situation had to be addressed for the good of the team. "He could do it because the kids trusted him," Hanlon said. "Those kids already knew that no one was more loyal to the program than Jon. They were afraid to go ask

Jon Falk and retired assistant coach Jerry Hanlon get together regularly and share stories from yesteryear.

him for another jock strap, but they trusted him. Once in a while, one of the coaches would run a message to a player through Jon. If you can handle that discreetly for 40 years, you must be doing a good job."

During his first season with Michigan in 1974, Falk was barely older than most of the players. It didn't bother Falk. And it certainly didn't bother Bo, who always remained confident after making a major decision. "Of course, it worked," Bo once snapped soon after he watched Falk operate. "I wouldn't have hired him if I hadn't felt confident he could handle the job." Falk still smiles at the way Bo made him feel he was an integral part of the team. "That's the way he treated everyone on the team," Falk said. "It was always about the team…the team…the team."

The locker room is more a state of mind and spirit than an oversized play room where uniforms and equipment are put on and taken off. The locker room is where individual attitudes are created and then nurtured for the good of the whole. It's where game plans are crafted and then mellowed to perfection. The locker room is where lifetime friendships are born and a commitment to Michigan is promised for life. It was in the locker room where Falk made his most meaningful contributions to the team.

As the man responsible for the day-to-day operation of the locker room, Falk learned to master that invisible tightrope between coaches and players. When internal problems arose, Falk had to devise a plan to share that issue with a coach without betraying his relationship with any player. "It can get sticky," Falk confirmed. "But we take great pride in here that everything is done for the good of the whole team. Not just an individual."

However a particular issue was handled, it always was done discreetly and honestly.

"Sometimes a player makes a mistake, and the coach has to be told about it," Falk explained. "When that player takes time to understand what he might have done, he usually appreciates the process that helps him to become a better man."

Certainly the players must have embraced that bond of trust. Falk still maintains all of the friendships he made over the years and appreciates the phone calls and visits from players from the past. "I can't imagine going back to Michigan without dropping in on Big Jon," said quarterback and four-time Super Bowl champion Tom Brady. "He's not only a friend; he's become a Michigan icon."

That friendship runs throughout the long line of Michigan alums. Now no longer players, but Michigan Men for life. That friendship always made Falk smile. It always made Falk recall a subtle, yet distinct memory made by Bo. Bo and his wife, Cathy, were driving US-23 North back to their Ann Arbor home late in the summer of 2006. They were returning from Columbus, Ohio, where Bo had been a guest of honor at an Ohio State football reunion the evening before. It was one of those sticky autumn afternoons that makes every ice cream truck driver smile. It also was one of the sure signs of the season that college football was only a few weeks from swallowing the entire sporting nation.

Bo and Cathy enjoyed a fabulously good time at the reunion. Former Buckeyes swarmed the Michigan legend as if Bo had coached the Scarlet and Gray instead of the Maize and Blue. They shook his hand, slapped him on the back, hugged him. They spoke with the same reverence in their voices that they had reserved for their coach, Woody Hayes, when he was roaming the sidelines or delivering a short lecture on world history.

And on the drive home, Bo wondered why.

Upon getting home, Bo called Falk to share the mystifying experience with his longtime confidante. "They treated me like royalty," Bo said. "You would have thought I was one of them."

Falk broke into a laugh that made Bo even more confused. "Don't you get it?" Falk asked his mentor and best friend. "In your own special way, you are one of them. Think about it. You're their last link to Woody. They know what you and Woody mean to both schools and how much you mean to college football. That 10-Year War that you and Woody fought so furiously will never happen again. All those guys at the banquet are proud of you. They just wore different color shirts than us and tried to knock our guys into next week."

When it comes to understanding a link to a legend, few have the perspective of Falk from both ends of the chain.

More than merely the practices and even the Saturday games, Falk misses the locker room camaraderie. He misses the banter. He misses the innocent, harmless horseplay that only a locker room allows. Most of all he misses the challenge of excellence that a football program such as the University of Michigan runs daily throughout the year.

Within the first month of the 2014 Detroit Tigers season, Falk attended a game against the Chicago White Sox at Comerica Park. He and White Sox trainer Herm Schneider are longtime friends. Cajoling with White Sox manager Robin Ventura and Adam Dunn on the field during batting practice, Falk was asked what he missed most from his official retirement. Falk smiled. His eyes wandered from the players on the field to all the fans seated in the colorful stadium. He shook his head and winked. Only a couple of months into retirement, Falk pointed at Chicago's dugout that has a runway to the locker room. "Right in there, Robin," he said. "Right in there. There's nothing like a locker room at any level. Doesn't matter if that room is big or if it's small. I miss it every day."

Chapter **5**
Knowing the Coaches

With about 125 players, around a dozen coaches, and a handful of trainers and medical personnel to serve each day, Jon Falk's schedule was
thoroughly filled throughout each day of the season. Now he's regarded as the
mayor emeritus of the locker room where former players and coaches still love
to visit him whenever possible. For those who live out of town, many keep in
contact through phone calls or emails. And the messages are countless.

And with longtime friend Jim Harbaugh at the football helm, Jon still
may be called upon to pull his magic to help solve some sticky matters that
arise in the clubhouse or practice fields.

Except for three years when he served as football assistant equipment
manager at Miami of Ohio, Falk spent his entire working career as the head
equipment manager for the University of Michigan. Same job. Same equipment. Same high expectations for excellence. Same passion for his team.
Without a doubt, Falk is the Cal Ripken Jr. of major college football. With
barely a handful of sick days taken along the way, Falk could serve as the
poster boy for institutional loyalty.

Falk's physical presence around Ann Arbor and the surrounding towns is a reassuring staple in Washtenaw County. Never one to worry about winning any fashion award, he'll forever be proud to wear the Michigan maize and blue. Just as he did when he was working full time in the locker room, each new day he still wears the same color workout suit with the rich Michigan navy blue and distinctive maize block "M" on the front of each item. In the fall and winter, he wears long nylon running pants and a matching Michigan jacket. He wears maize and blue shorts and T-shirts in the summer and spring. And no day passes without him sporting that distinctive maize and blue block M baseball cap with just the right fold of the visor.

For 40 years he's been a walking, talking billboard for Michigan wherever he happens to wander. With his size and frame of an NFL defensive end, everyone knows when Big Jon is around. "That's a sign of how deeply Jon is ingrained into the fabric of the university and particularly the football team," Rich Rodriguez said. "When recruiting and we needed just the right man to share the Michigan story and all of its traditions, we had Big Jon talk to the recruits. These are young high school kids, and they could feel the passion in his voice."

There are a lot of similarities between the last five football head coaches and now sixth with Harbaugh at the University of Michigan. Falk is the only staff member to have served all of them.

- All hold a respectful disdain for Ohio State.
- All enjoy stuffing a football down the throats of any opponent.
- All appreciate the numerous yardsticks of tradition that only Michigan enjoys.
- All are quite convinced that no other major college football equipment manager will have a tenure measured in decades rather than merely years.

"I don't think you'll ever see another one quite like Big Jon," Brady Hoke said. "Forty years at any job today is a rarity in our society. But in the high-profile and volatile world of big-time college football, that record may not ever be reached again. Big Jon just loves the football program so much. He's so ingrained into it. He understands all of the nuances that go into serving the coaches and the players. There are a lot of different personalities and egos in that locker room. Jon had a way of touching them all."

The title of equipment manager falls a football field too short for describing all of Falk's responsibilities. Lloyd Carr once described him as a "locker room coach" because he served as the bridge between the coaches and the players. Because Falk spent so much time in the locker room, he always had the pulse of a team. During the season and during the offseason, Falk was one of the first to arrive in the locker room and get the coffee brewing. He also was one of the last men out and the first ready to go back again the next morning.

Because of his omnipresence and loyalty to the program, he was trusted by the entire staff and all the players who built the program into what it is today. "We've run into some glitches now, but they'll get straightened out soon, and Michigan will be back to being the program where it ought to be," Falk said.

Falk never betrayed a confidence. But if a possible situation of concern was brewing in the locker room, Falk knew how to discreetly get a message to the coaches in order to quell the problem before it got out of hand. "You had to love Big Jon," Rodriguez said. "He was a counselor to the players and a confidante of the coaches. He's such a positive guy when it comes to Michigan. He's an extension of the coaching staff…a true ambassador for the entire football program. I don't think there's a person in Ann Arbor that doesn't know him. At least by looks and that infectious laugh, that is truly one of a kind. He always has time for sharing a few moments with people who are looking for a few words."

Gary Moeller worked with Falk as a head coach and an assistant. Mo also spent time coaching in the National Football League. He's familiar with equipment managers at every level. Mo felt he received the same treatment from Falk that Bo did. "As a head coach, you don't want to get caught by an equipment problem," Mo said. "That can throw a whole week into a mess.

You never worried about that with Jon. He was precise with every assignment. You never had to worry about him trying to take a shortcut."

Moeller remains grateful for how Falk adapted to suit the program Mo instituted when he was elevated to head coach. "He made my transition to head coach so easy," Mo said. "Some members of the staff have a difficult time doing that. Jon knew what the job entailed and made it easy for me and the entire staff."

Brady Hoke first worked with Falk in 1995 when he served as an assistant under Carr. He knew when he took the Michigan job that he wouldn't have to worry about clubhouse matters with Falk there. "The credit for treating staff members properly goes back to Bo," Falk said. "Bo made sure that every staff member be treated as a professional. Each role is critical for championship teams. Hoke said Jon was able to anticipate solutions to any problems to help anyone on the coaching staff."

Brady Hoke needed a specific type of blocking sled for practices. "I mentioned it to Jon, and it seems like that sled showed up the next day," Hoke said. "He takes great pride in being part of the Michigan program."

"If there's another guy like Falk out there, I'd like to see him," Rodriguez said. "But I know that guy wouldn't stick around for 40 years."

That's just Jon Falk. He took great pride in learning the personalities of all the coaches he served. "Bo expected each member of the staff to understand his personal role in the program Bo designed," Falk said. "It was a simple program that demanded precision, dedication, and commitment."

Moeller certainly appreciated the precision of Falk's role in the program. "What really sticks out in my mind with Jon is the fact that he was ready to deal with any type of unforeseen problem," Moeller said. "That's the last kind of situation any head coach wants to deal with as the gameday drew closer."

Carr was always impressed with Falk's attention to detail. "He knew what his job was and never was late with anything," Carr said. "A head coach has to depend on the equipment manager for so many details, and Jon never let us down."

Jon Falk has known Brady Hoke since the coach served as an assistant under Lloyd Carr in 1995.

Rodriguez echoed the sentiments of all of his predecessors. "I had a whole lot to learn when I first got to Ann Arbor," Rodriguez said. "Jon took the time to familiarize me with so much history. He is truly a very unselfish man."

From the coach's time under Carr, Falk already knew what to expect from Hoke. And Falk also took great pride in learning each coach's personality. "There's nothing more rewarding for any equipment manager than to be able to tell the head coach that something was already done before anyone had to worry about it," Falk said.

Chapter **6**
The Prime Seat

Rarely is a man fortunate enough to serve as the right-hand-man of a legitimate history-making legend. And almost never is he afforded that good fortune for the 16 years they worked together in the locker room and on the field. That's a hearty bite out of the 40 years Falk spent at the university. And it's one that no other equipment manager is likely ever to taste again.

After each home and road game throughout the '70s and '80s after Bo had addressed the media, Falk and Bo sat alone in the coach's office dissecting the good, the not-so-good, and all the in-between of that day's performance. Actually, it was Bo who did most of the talking. And when Bo spoke, everyone listened.

Those talks were the ultimate expression of the friendship and trust the two shared with each other. "I still find it hard to believe that a boy from Oxford, Ohio, could have had the experience of sitting alone with Bo after a game talking football," Falk said. "Bo is more than a Michigan legend. He's an all-time coaching legend. A maker of men...not just football players."

Falk would listen intently to every word. Right there in that moment, Falk could see the beginning of a game plan for the following Saturday springing to life in Bo's eyes. Of course, Falk knew for sure it would include a lot of smashmouth running straight up the middle. He might have planned a surprise or two depending upon the opponent. But exploding holes in the offensive and defensive lines is what Bo loved best. "There was no one else like Bo," Falk said. "Not at the college level. Not at the professional level. Bo demanded discipline because he had disciplined himself. He's one of only a handful throughout history. No one needs to hear his last name. The sound of 'Bo' says it all."

Falk was the lone man on the football staff to have served the last five football head coaches. Following Bo were Gary Moeller, Lloyd Carr, Rich Rodriguez, Brady Hoke, and now Jim Harbaugh. But their success at Michigan all began with Bo. And even from afar, Rodriguez was wise enough to have learned a lot from Bo. "Looking back now, I truly appreciate the honor of having had that experience of learning from Bo," Falk said. "This was a man who could almost will his way to victory. He was the force that brought Michigan football back to glory. And any coach that follows at the University of Michigan will always feel the impact of his legacy."

Bo devised a master plan when he took the Michigan job in 1969. He designed it. He refined it. He made adjustments to adapt to an opponent's strengths and weaknesses. But he never wandered from the program that he knew he could drive to victory. "Bo was the kind of guy who had blind faith in the program of his design," Falk said. "And all the coaches and players understood that they better get with Bo's program or they would be getting nowhere at all. He listened to his coaches and even implemented some of their suggestions. But those ideas better not have wandered too far from his overall vision."

Bo was a disciplinarian who expected the same commitment from his coaches and players that he imposed upon himself. If he called for a 9:00 AM team meeting, players were expected to be assembled by 8:45—sometimes

8:30 just to make sure if the previous Saturday's overall play lacked the crispness Bo demanded of his team. "Bo believed that every player, once in a while, secretly wanted a kick in the butt," Falk said. "They may not like it at the time, but after they graduate and have a few years to reflect upon their football careers, they appreciate what Bo had done for them in the long run—both on the field and off. Some look back and wish they had worked a little harder or had done a little more for their team. But at least they finally got the message. They finally learned the lesson that the discipline Bo had instilled in them as young players could finally be put to use for success in the real world. That's why Bo was tough. And the men he made now understand."

What a lot of people don't appreciate is that Bo also had a sense of humor that cut to the bone. When Don Nehlen was appointed to be the quarterback coach, a story in one of the Detroit newspapers said he was hired to develop more of a passing game. Falk read the story and brought it to Bo before the morning staff meeting. "What's this story I read in the paper this morning?" Bo said to Nehlen. "What's all this stuff about a passing game coming to Michigan? Let me explain something simple and straight right now. At Michigan we run the ball. Then we run it again. And just to make sure everyone knows how the game is supposed to be played, we run it again." By this time all the assistant coaches and Falk were having trouble holding back a smile. Finally, Bo looked at Falk and winked. Then everyone broke into a little laugh…especially Nehlen, who got the message.

Each head coach has his own way of running his program. Mo thought a little differently than Carr and so on down the line. "My success for lasting as long as I did was the fact that I was able to change with each one by figuring out how each one thought," Falk said. "I was able to blend into their programs and their sense of discipline. Each coach has a different philosophy about how to treat players. By learning a coach's mode of operation, I was able to become a better equipment manager."

Bo was precise with the way he selected assistant coaches. He liked those unafraid to express their convictions. He welcomed fresh ideas. Bo knew the coaches. He understood how each one operated and how that man would fit into Bo's vision. "Don't ever tell me what a man can't do," Bo emphasized. "Tell me what he can do and then make him do it. Let's not try to make a man do something he can't. Let's put him into a position where he can succeed."

When Bo retired he handpicked Moeller to be his successor. Moeller was one of Bo's assistants and learned his fundamentals from playing for Woody Hayes at Ohio State. Moeller was football smart. He was one of the country's most successful recruiters and did—in fact—open up a little more of a passing attack to make the offense more versatile.

Having recruited quarterback Elvis Grbac and wide receiver Desmond Howard out of Ohio made the decision to incorporate a lethal passing attack an easy one and one that could not be ignored. The running attack still had to be explosively consistent, but the ball began to fly more at The Big House.

Having to follow Bo as head coach at Michigan had to be a daunting assignment that only Moeller could truly feel—sort of like being the successor to Charles Woodson at cornerback. If somehow the university could have brought Fielding Yost back from his grave, even he would have had a problem following those giant footprints that Bo left. "Mo came in carrying a lot of pressure on his shoulders," Falk said. "He was following a legend. Only he could really feel the weight."

Watching over Moeller, Falk observed that the coach interacted more with the players than did Bo. "Not to say that Bo didn't, but Mo listened a little more to suggestions from the assistants and sometimes the players, too," Falk said. "Bo had a master plan and didn't let anything get in the way."

Because of the way Bo raised all of his coaches, Falk was part of all staff meetings. He instilled credibility into every member of the staff. "That was an honor and made my job a lot easier," Falk said. "It really made me feel part of the team. Mo was more of a listener than Bo was, but in the end, Mo made the final decision."

Falk had known Carr for several years before he was elevated to head coach in 1995. In fact, the two roomed together in Falk's small apartment on the university's golf course upon his arrival. That made Carr's promotion to head coach easier for Falk. "We were friends," Falk said. "I learned a lot from Lloyd. Lloyd taught me the virtue of persistence. That's the way he always conducted himself. He remained calm in a storm. He taught me the importance of being tolerant yet still be forceful in the way you handle yourself." Falk believes Carr is the most well-read person he has ever encountered in football. "He read more books in one season than I did in my 40 years," Falk said. "He liked inspirational books that he could share with the players and everyone on the staff. He's a very intelligent man."

Falk remains good friends with Carr and Moeller, who continue to live in the Ann Arbor area. They still get enjoyment from reminiscing about the "old times." "I value their judgment on a lot of important matters," Falk said. "In fact, those were the first two people I talked to when I was considering retirement. I knew I could rely on their opinions. Both supported me in making the biggest decision of my career. They said 40 years is an awful long time at a place like the University of Michigan. They reminded me how lucky I have been. And they're right."

The hiring of RichRod remains a conundrum in the history of Michigan football. It's probably going to take a while longer before all the pieces finally unfold and then get put back together to truly understand the three-year tenure of Rodriguez as head coach.

Some of the hardcore Michigan fanatics maintain that an outsider coming from West Virginia was a misfit for the Michigan family. Others disagree and believe that he deserved more than three years for his program to mature, considering the caliber of players he inherited and those he recruited to fill the offense and defense. Some maintain that Rodriguez played a lot of players out of position for the wide-open game he has employed throughout his entire career. Others disagree and believe that it takes a handful of years for any coach to stock his roster with the specialty players needed to run such an intricate offense. Whatever the case may be, the three years with Rodriguez as head coach will take at least double that amount of time for all wounds to heal. "And that's too bad because RichRod is a good man and didn't really get the opportunity to get his program going," Falk said. "Mo and Lloyd have different personalities than what RichRod has. Of course, there were bound to be philosophic differences. That's the right each head coach has."

Falk was careful not to take sides in the "great debate." He did wonder, however, how Bo would have handled the situation had he been around. "I kept running it through my mind," Falk said. "What would Bo have done? What would he have had suggested that I do? I came to the conclusion he would have told me that my job was to serve Rich in the same way I had served the three head coaches that preceded him. He was head coach of the University of Michigan football team and was accorded all the support he needed to do the best job he could."

Falk became a confidante of Rodriguez and wound up trying to make the coach understand more about Michigan tradition. For instance, Rodriguez loved locker room signage that promoted teamwork. As he did at West Virginia, he used the phrase "Hold the Rope" on a plaque in the locker room to promote team unity. Falk explained that the "Go Blue Go" sign had been used for years. He then coupled both phrases together into one and hung it over the locker room door. Rodriguez perceived that as an attempt to blend the past with the present. But blending the past with that present wasn't enough and he was dismissed after three years.

On Rodriguez's last day at Michigan, Falk visited the dejected coach. "I wanted to tell Rich two quick things," Falk said. "I wanted to be able to say that I did everything I could to help Michigan and Rich Rodriguez. Secondly, I wanted Rich Rodriguez to be able to say that Jon Falk did everything he could to help me when he did walk out that door." Rodriguez rose from his chair and came around the desk to hug Falk. "You did everything you could to help me here," Rodriguez said. "I thank you very much."

Falk holds a simple perspective about the condition of the Michigan program. "Bo, Mo, and Lloyd recruited the same type of players—strong and

Jon Falk hangs out with Rich Rodriguez, who served as Michigan's head coach for just three years, at the ballpark.

nasty," Falk said. "To run the program the way it was traditionally run, we need that kind of players. When Rodriguez came in, he recruited kids with speed who could open up the field. When you change a whole system, it takes time to get the right players in the right places. The players we used to recruit for our style of play started going to Michigan State and Notre Dame and Ohio State. They ran the same kind of offense that we used to run. As soon as Rich left, I predicted it's going to take six years for Michigan to get back to where we were. You just can't come back and expect everything to fall into place. Now with Michigan-bred Harbaugh in charge, it's expected that old-fashioned hitting will play a more vital role in the success of the team. Time will be needed to get the right pieces to fill in the holes. But we must get all the pieces together and prove that Michigan can bounce back. I believe in Michigan. We will be back! The problem is that we live in a give-it-to-me-now society. Not next week. Not even tomorrow. We want everything today. Michigan will be back. Maybe even stronger than before. Just give it a little time."

Chapter **7**

Retirement

I n his masterful tribute to Bo—*Bo's Lasting Lessons*—celebrated author John U. Bacon tenderly captures the essence of retirement, according to Bo.

"Someday someone is going to take your job, and you're going to have to let them," Bo said. "If you became a leader for the right reasons in the first place, you'll be able to pass it on and feel good about it. When I announced my retirement in 1989, I knew we had a hell of a team coming back the next season. And I'm not going to lie to you: I would have loved to coach that team. We had everything! And if it wasn't for my ticker, I would have. But my doctor made it clear I was pushing it as it was, and, if I wanted to spend more good years with my family, I had to get out. Lord knows I owed them that.

"But I didn't just say good-bye and walk out the door. Like Bump did for me, I left the cupboard full. I wanted to set up my successor, Gary Moeller, for success. So I prepared our people to make that transition work. Before we made it official, Gary invited me to stay on as

the front man while he and the other assistants did the actual work. That was a very generous gesture, to say the least. But I couldn't do it because it wouldn't be honest. I can feel good that every day I was on the job I gave everything I had. I never wanted to compromise that or the program we all had worked so hard to build up. It was time for me to go.

"By promoting Gary, we not only got a great coach, we got to ensure that everyone else could stay on, too—the assistants, the train- ers, the secretaries. Everybody. In fact, that was the only condition I had when I left: If I step down, only one guy is leaving—and his name is Schembechler!"

It wasn't easy for Falk to step down from the very position that defined him either. Forty years in any single place is a lifetime. With the pitfalls and perils of performing flawlessly behind the scenes of a demanding public, the position engenders a life of its own. "I can't imagine doing anything more satisfying than what I did for the last four decades," Falk said. "Everything just chugged down those tracks a whole lot quicker than what I would have liked. And the train waits for no one."

Running even quicker, however, were radical changes throughout the athletic department after Dave Brandon was named athletic director. Obviously, some of those changes and an unexpected rash of marketing gimmickry that diluted the romance of Michigan tradition also affected the equipment manager's position. And after long discussions with his wife, Cheri, and reflections on the advice that Bo had instilled into him, Big Jon decided it was time for him to retire.

Jon and Cheri were on a northern Michigan vacation when she reminded him that he had promised Brandon a full year's notice before stepping into retirement. On July 14, 2013 at 7:30 AM, Falk visited Brandon's office to com- plete his promise. The deal was agreed upon by both sides, and it was done. Falk would retire at a mutually agreed upon date in 2014.

Perhaps even more important to Falk was that he would be allowed to run the locker room the same way he had been doing for 40 years until after participation in any bowl game in the early part of the year. And most important was the assurance that his assistants would be retained to work under the new equipment manager. Falk agreed to go on all 2013 road trips and to use these trips as a part of his "farewell tour."

On July 21, Falk informed Brady Hoke and former head coaches Gary Moeller and Lloyd Carr of his decision. At the team meeting on the first day of fall practice in 2013, Hoke informed the players, the assistant coaches, and the entire football staff that Falk would be leaving after the season. "There's a man in this room here who has been at Michigan for 40 years," Hoke began. "He's helped Michigan win football championships throughout those 40 years. He's going be retiring after the end of this season. I know this much for sure: Michigan is going miss him and so will I."

As Falk walked to the front of the room, the team exploded into a round of heartfelt applause. By the time he reached the front of the room, tears already were trickling down his cheeks…and also down some cheeks of the players, too. "On the way to that podium, I wondered where those 40 years had gone and how quickly they flew by," Falk said. "So many images. So many things that I had learned along the way."

This type of locker room good-bye is atypical for an equipment manager. But this was not a typical good-bye. This one was designed specifically for Big Jon. Most players thought Falk would be delivering his annual little speech of how the locker room would operate throughout the season. They thought they would be getting their first rally speech of the season. Suddenly, though, tears began to stream down the cheeks of the players, who rose to a standing position. "To have the players give me a standing ovation was really special," Falk said. "This is the kind of honor that is usually reserved for a head coach leaving. I stood in the back of the room when Bo said good-bye. I did the same thing for Mo and Lloyd and RichRod. Or maybe an All-American speaking before his senior year. I never dreamed I'd be standing on this side of the room with a microphone in my hand."

As his eyes moved slowly around the entire room, Falk could visualize and even feel the presence of all the players he had served for four decades. He felt the fierce spirit of Bo. He sensed the presence of Curtis Greer and Rick Leach and Anthony Carter and the Dufek brothers and Jake Long and Charles Woodson and Desmond Howard and Anthony Thomas and Rob Lytle and Denard Robinson and Tom Brady and Braylon Edwards and Chad Henne.

There were so many more. It seemed as if the entire Michigan football family somehow had managed to pack the room…at least in spirit. "I wanted to thank and hug each one," Falk said. "I told them how much Michigan has meant to me. I told them I was like a senior playing his last season here. The only difference is that it took me 40 years to graduate. Most of you do it in four, five, or maybe six years."

Then Falk challenged all the players to play hard each day to win another ring for Michigan. "Ask yourself each day," he said, "*What have I done today to help my team win a championship for Michigan?* If you go out there and play Michigan football every time your shoe hits the ground, I'll feel so proud."

Afterward, a lot of the former Michigan players must have flooded the airwaves with tweets and emails about Falk's announcement because messages from former players and coaches and friends from the entire sporting world bombarded Falk with messages of gratitude and best wishes for his retirement in the future.

A posse of former players who still live in the nearby area drove to Ann Arbor within the next couple of days to talk to Falk. They wanted to see if what they had heard was true. "Chris Perry came in crying," Falk said. "He asked who was he gonna come see anymore. [He said:] 'You're my man, Big Jon. Always will be.'" Ed Muransky made a special effort to get a special retirement gift to Big Jon.

Just as life changes in the real world, so too does it change in sports. Falk recalled what Bo once told him after he retired. "Nobody got me," Bo said.

Wolverines fan and former Detroit Tigers star Alan Trammell jokes that Jon Falk has been with Michigan since the Fielding Yost era.

"Nobody had to call me in. Nobody put pressure on me. Retiring is not the same as quitting. You just always want to remember that when you leave a job for retirement that the job is left in better shape than it was when you took it."

Falk took Bo's words to heart and practiced them throughout his career. "That's the way I viewed the equipment manager job at Michigan," Falk said. "I never threw or caught a pass, never knocked an opponent into the middle of next week. But I definitely felt that the locker room and the position of equipment manager was in better shape after I left than it was when I first took the job."

To finish his address to the players after his announcement and with a whimsical wink of the eye to Frank Sinatra, Falk left with this tidbit of wisdom. "But now, the end is here, and I must face the final curtain," he began. "My friends, I'll make it clear and state my case of which I'm certain.

I've lived a life that's full and travelled each and every highway. But more, much more than this, I can proudly say I did it the Michigan way."

By the time Falk reached his final words, every person in the room had a tear in each eye.

Falk is wise enough to know that leaving his lifelong dream job was bound to create a few ripples throughout the world of major college football. He just didn't realize how those ripples would quickly turn into waves of gratitude and congratulations from colleagues and friends from throughout the country and all the people he has touched.

Those messages came from former football players, former football coaches, Major League Baseball managers, baseball players, and from an uncountable number of University of Michigan alumni and a loyal army of Michigan fans. "It's tough to understand how they can still play football at Michigan without Big Jon being there," said record-setting Detroit Tigers shortstop Alan Trammell.

Trammell is part of a Major League Baseball longevity record himself. He and second baseman Lou Whitaker combined in the keystone positions for an unprecedented 19 seasons. Trammell and Falk have been friends for decades. It seems like all of the truly good teams, regardless of the sport, have a character like Jon Falk, Trammell said. "Big Jon takes his loyalty to another level," Trammell added, "seems like he's been there since Fielding Yost. And he sure does love that university. He's a once-in-a-lifetime guy when it comes to college football."

Chapter **8**
Tradition

"I've always maintained that for being considered such a liberal institution, the University of Michigan is more conservative than a black suit and wing-tip shoes," said Jon Falk, whose 40 years in the football program made him somewhat of a conservative tradition himself.

Like every officer, administrator, faculty member, and coach, Falk is proud of the intellectual giant that has often been rated the No. 1 public university in the country. The faculty is world-acclaimed. Research is robust. The international body of students revels in its intellectual curiosity. And Michigan's collection of various individual and team championships is a kaleidoscope of athletic excellence, which is more than a century old. The balance between athletic excellence and academic achievement is a long-lived standard.

But even a storybook football tradition such as at Michigan needs a little wake-up call from the last few years. The departure of two head coaches, a pair of coaching staffs, and one athletic director have drastically challenged the foundation of one of college football's most stable institutions. But one result of the public outcry for the return of tradition to the proud history of football is particularly encouraging to Falk. "Even today's young students don't want to surrender that storied tradition of Michigan football," Falk said. "They appreciate the tradition upon which the football program is founded and embraced. It's too valuable to simply let it slip away. And now with Jim Harbaugh and Jim Hackett on board, true fans need not worry."

Falk is convinced that today's students prefer blending the tradition of those precious Saturdays past with those of the present to create new traditions. They're discerning with their purchasing power and demanding that time-honored traditions remain untouched for future generations. "In a lot of ways, they want to go back to the way it used to be at Michigan," Falk said. "They don't like all the commercialism of the last couple of years. They don't want to sacrifice all the traditions that have become the very fabric of Michigan football. They don't like all of the commercial sideshows and gimmicks."

Students are savvy enough to realize part of the money raised by commercialism underwrites the entire football program and parts of all the sports. But there are certain traditions that ought to be held above all others for new generations to be held sacred. Legendary coach and athletic director Fritz Crisler said it best: "Tradition is something you can't bottle. You can't buy it at the corner store. But it is there to sustain you when you need it most. I've called upon it time and time again. And so have countless other Michigan athletes and coaches. There is nothing like it. I hope it never dies."

As an example of that everlasting Michigan tradition, Falk believes that not only the students, but also Michigan graduates and weekend warrior fans want those same maize and blue uniforms to complement the most distinctive helmet in the game. "Fans pay a pretty price to watch a game in The Big House," Falk said. "When they show up, they want to look down from the stands at the stadium and appreciate that this is Michigan. I think all those recent uniform changes have turned a lot of people off. A lot of students and faculty members are liberal in their political beliefs. But they want

Jon Falk taps the famous sign before proceeding down the Tunnel for his final game as Michigan equipment manager.

those maize and blue colors all over the place when they get to the stadium for game days. They treasure that tradition. When they go to a game, they want to see Michigan! They want to feel Michigan!"

Falk had to fight some last-second "hold your breath moments" just before gametime because of all the uniform changes that no one appeared to like, especially the players and most of all the fans. One incident occurred at Michigan State in 2011. Michigan players ran through their pregame drills in regular uniforms. Unbeknownst to the players, specially designed uniforms were waiting for them in the locker room for the start of the game.

And the players were not happy.

Some of the pants did not fit them the way their regular uniforms did. Fortunately, Falk had brought extra uniforms to cover all the sizes. Center David Molk's pants fit so tight Falk had to take a pair of scissors to cut the seams in his rear in order for him to lean over enough to snap the ball properly.

A similar situation at the Sugar Bowl that same season created an even bigger problem. Fifteen of the jerseys were unusable because they didn't fit. "I had to call the seamstress for the New Orleans Saints to come in and let out all 15," Falk said. "When you change jerseys like that, you change the way the players play. They get used to the fitting of their particular jersey. They're comfortable the way they are cut. The sleeves on all jerseys are cut differently today. Every position has a separate sleeve size and tightness."

And that added tightness on today's uniform is another change that affects the players of all positions. Falk explained that today's players want their uniforms tight. "They want to feel that the uniforms are part of the players' skin," he said. "It makes it tougher for defensive players to get a firm hold on an opponent.' It also shows off all the muscles that result from all that weightlifting."

Every coach wants his players to feel as comfortable as possible when they run out onto the field for the start of a new game. Every coach and every equipment manager keeps his eye open for any new piece of equipment that will enhance a player's performance.

Falk said uniforms started to get tighter when Bo was the coach. "Bo said we were losing too many yards with players grabbing the jerseys and tackling our guys," Falk said. "We used to have jerseys that were cut straight down. So we began putting elastic in the sides of the jerseys so they could cling to the sides of the players. They would cling to the shoulder pads and then to the player's body. Today they're so tight it's almost impossible to bring a guy down with a hand tackle to the jersey."

Falk said he started making jerseys tighter in the late '80s, and now schools across the country are doing the same thing. Butch Woolfolk was a bruising running back who hurt his ribs in 1981. Bo was concerned and called Falk into his office. "Now, Jon," the concerned coach began, "you know I want Woolfolk ready to play Saturday. What are you going to do about that?"

Falk was prepared with a suggestion. Bo never was the kind of person to dismiss any issue before getting a possible solution. "I can get a new pair of rib pads that the manufacturer just came out with," Falk said proudly, "claims the pads can take a direct hit from a train."

Bo, of course, made a spontaneous decision. "I don't care about any train," Bo said. "Just make sure it's linebacker and safeties-proof."

Falk received the rib pads the next morning and buckled them to his ribs and chest before walking into the coaches' meeting room, where everyone waited. He carried a baseball bat and dropped it on the table where Bo sat.

"Here, Bo," Falk said with a heavy dose of anxiety. "Take a shot." Bo lightly tapped on both sides of Falk's ribs a couple of times. And while Falk crossed his fingers, Bo then took a swing with the fury of one by Reggie Jackson.

All the coaches watched anxiously as Falk's feet stuck to the floor. The impact sprung Falk's head back. His teeth rattled like his tongue was playing a piano. But he said he felt no pain. "I think all of my teeth are chipped, but my ribs feel real good," Falk said.

Woolfolk used the pads for the game and for most of the rest of the season, and the ribs never felt better. The pads became Woolfolk's personal little slice of tradition that he used for the rest of his playing days.

Another great running back, Tyrone Wheatley, now a Michigan coach, came in one day and wanted smaller shoulder pads because the others were too big and bulky. But Falk cautioned that the team couldn't afford for him to be hurt. He looked at Jon and said, "I want smaller pads. The ones I have are slowing me up."

After a discussion of a few minutes and a couple of days of deliberation, Falk finally gave in and got him those shoulder pads, but the veteran equipment manager had a message: "If you get hurt and you're laying on the ground, I'm going to walk over to you and stand over the top of you and say 'Hey, Tyrone, I told you so.'"

That afternoon, he wore the small pads out for practice. Almost on cue,

Tyrone was laying on the ground. Falk walked over and asked what happened. The trainer said he hurt his shoulder. "I walked over to Tyrone," Falk said, "and he looked up at me and said, 'Please Jon, don't tell me, I told you so.' I said, 'Alright, but I want you to come in tomorrow and get bigger shoulder pads.' He did and still was the fastest weapon on any college football field."

Chapter **9**

History of the Gameday Banner

As the Michigan players get off the team bus that takes them to the stadium from the team hotel on a Saturday morning, a sense of unity surrounds this band of dedicated athletes. With determination they walk to the locker room, where they dress and head down the Tunnel for pregame warm-ups.

As the team heads back up the Tunnel to the locker room, the band is in the Tunnel ready to take the field. They jostle upward toward that curiously celebrated collection of athletes. Members of the band begin to shout "Let's Go Blue…Let's Go Blue." And as the echoes of the din blasts gloriously toward the field, the drums beat to the rhythm: "Let's Go Blue…Let's Go Blue."

They continue the same chant until it's ready to proudly take the field. The controlled commotion continues as players sit in seats strategically placed in front of a chalkboard. The assistant coaches review some of the plays they have integrated into this week's strategy, and anxiety continues to sizzle. Now the head coach walks in and orders the players to take a knee around him. The coach tells the players when they put on that uniform they do so to represent every Michigan football team that has played before them. When they put on that helmet, they do so for every player that ever played before them. Then that head coach looks each player in the eyes as he tells them, "You play hard…you play your best…you play for Michigan. The team across the field not only has to play the football team, it must play against the whole University of Michigan." The team proceeds through the Tunnel. As they near the door, they see a sign on top that says, "Go Blue…Go."

Each player taps that sign before proceeding down that tunnel, and then the light hits them in the face as they enter the field. With the band still playing "Let's Go Blue," the players look up to see 110,000 fans on their feet screaming for Michigan. As the team heads for the bench, the M club holds a banner that says "GO BLUE M CLUB SUPPORTS YOU." The players all jump to touch that banner and run toward the bench, where they are greeted by all the players, coaches, and staff members who are privileged to do so.

The tradition started in 1962 when the late former Michigan hockey coach Al Renfrew and his late wife, Marge, were determined to add more spice to the entry. Both are deceased, but their inspiring tradition still lives on.

Marge made 20 Michigan flags and had former Michigan players stand on each side of the 50-yard line and wave the flags as the team ran between them. The M club saw this and said they wanted the football team to know that all Michigan letter winners support their team. So a banner made in 1963 said "GO BLUE M CLUB SUPPORTS YOU." All varsity M club winners hold that banner as the team runs and jumps to tap the banner. The banner was held like this until 1973, when the Ohio State University players tore the banner down. To put it in Bob Ufer's words, "Here come the Buckeyes, and they're tearing down Michigan's coveted M club banner. They will meet a ghastly fate here today. There isn't a Michigan man alive who wouldn't want to go out and scalp those Buckeyes right now. They had the audacity, the unmitigated gall to tear down the Michigan's coveted

The Michigan players tap the famous banner, a tradition that dates back to the early 1960s. (Courtesy University of Michigan Athletic Department)

M club banner. But the men from Michigan are prevailing because they're getting their banner back up. And here comes the maize and blue. Take it over Michigan. We love you from coast to coast…the coast of Lake Erie to the coast of Lake Michigan!"

"In 1975 we played OSU at home," Jon Falk said. "When we took the field, we looked up around the M Go Blue banner where all the former players who ever played at Michigan were there to protect that banner to make sure that the OSU players were not going to take it down this year. The next day there was a picture in the paper that showed a Michigan man wearing his letter jacket and grabbing Woody Hayes while Woody had a hold of him underneath the banner. I showed it to Coach Schembechler and said, 'Look at this, I didn't know they had a problem yesterday at the banner.' Bo looked at it and said, 'Who is that guy that has a hold of Woody?' I said, 'That's Dave

Gallagher, former captain of the Michigan team.' Bo laughed and said, 'They made sure Woody wasn't going to get the banner this year, didn't they?'"

In 1998, the Friday before the Syracuse game, the banner was laid out in Crisler Arena on the basketball court. The next day when students arrived to get the M club banner, it was gone. Someone had stolen the M club banner from Crisler Arena. So before the football game, the M club members all lined up along the 50-yard line so that the players could run between them. As the players took the field, there was no banner to be touched. But many players were jumping anyway as if the banner was there.

The players were disoriented, and things did not feel right. Donovan McNabb, the quarterback for Syracuse, and his team built a 24–0 lead before Michigan could even score. The final score was 38–28 Syracuse. The players never recovered from not having the banner to touch. We made a make-shift banner until a good one was prepared. But the GO BLUE M CLUB SUPPORTS YOU banner is still held today by all Michigan men and women and Michigan club members.

What a privilege it is to run down the Tunnel and touch that banner, what an honor to play for Michigan, the best academic and athletic college in the country. People, who watch the players come out of the Tunnel, do not realize all the work that the players had to do to get down that tunnel. They don't know what's behind that tunnel. What they do realize is the pride and tradition that's behind there.

Chapter **10**

Recruiting

After retiring, Bo enjoyed spending just the right amount of time in his modest office in Schembechler Hall, especially during the football seasons. Not the entire day. Sometimes only a couple of hours. Just long enough to get all the inside dope about his beloved Michigan team as well as well as carving out as much time as needed to handle visits and phone calls from his former players and coaches.

Bo always made time to visit with them.

Once in a while Lloyd Carr would wander down to Bo's office just to pick the brain of the master or maybe share a memory of a game played long ago. Throughout the year, but especially during the football season, a lot of former players returned merely to say hello to their revered mentor who had set them on the right track for life. Bo loved those visits. These were the boys he had turned into men. He always had time to carve out for them. Bo remembered all the names, their positions, their numbers, a couple of critical playing highlights that may have turned a game or two around, and sometimes even the professions they had chosen in life.

Of course, those same players always took time to stop in the locker room to share some special memories that only a college football locker room can generate. And there was no better character to swap those stories with than Big Jon. In spite of his retirement, he was—and remains—the official custodian of all Michigan football memories and traditions.

With Falk no longer there at Michigan in a full-time position, so many of those precious stories teeter on the brink of complete obscurity. Sometimes a trip down memory lane proves to be even more rewarding, and another precious memory springs to life. Just as Bo did, Falk prides himself on remembering all the names, numbers, and faces of those mostly happy memories along with a few character-building sad ones. "No former player would ever go to Ann Arbor without stopping by to see Big Jon in the locker room," former quarterback Rick Leach said. "That would be a crime…first degree. Big Jon was always ready to welcome a former player into the locker room. And that player would feel twice as good when it was time to leave."

Falk always cherished a visit from a familiar face. In fact, he came to expect it. That's the magic of the locker room…and of Big Jon Falk. By the time Bo retired, Falk had become as much of a fixture in the football program as the stadium tunnel that links the locker room to the sacred football field.

Falk used to walk up from his locker room office in Schembechler Hall a couple of times a day just to see how Bo was doing and get in a couple of good-natured jabs, as best friends like to do. "I used to tease him that he couldn't coach the team today like he used to back in the '70s and '80s," Falk chuckled. "The landscape's changed too much."

Bo's spontaneous outburst, of course, was humorously retaliatory. "First thing I'd have to do would be to find an equipment manager," Bo fired back, "someone to take your spot."

After a few more good-natured barbs bounced back and forth, Bo would look sternly at Falk and conceded: "You just might be right, Falk…you just might be right."

Falk's contention is based on the fact that today's players aren't the same as they were when Bo coached. And neither is the college football landscape, which has morphed into one of the biggest corporate gold mines in the history of sports. As society continues to change, so too do the student-athletes, who are privileged to play major college football. That doesn't make them better at the game, and it doesn't make them worse. It just makes them different from those who played before they did. They're simply not the same," Falk said. "Everything has been corporatized. "That doesn't make 'em bad. But even Bo would have a little trouble trying to make sense out of the direction the big-time teams have chosen to follow."

The amount of social changes between today and when Bo coached is immeasurable. And some of those changes do affect the players on the field. They affect every position in life. The technological revolution that has changed the way we communicate with others is one of the most significant. It's fascinating even to ponder how Bo would have handled this revolutionary phenomenon with his players. "It's hard to keep up with all the methods of communication we have now," Falk said. "Tweets. Blogs. Who knows what's coming next? It used to be that something might happen out on the West Coast that affects our program here, and we wouldn't get the news until the next day. Now kids can send all that stuff all over the world the moment they get the news from someone else. And sometimes it gets to the players just before the opening kickoff. The social media has gotten bigger and bigger...and not necessarily better than what it was before."

All coaches today have to adapt to situations no one had even dreamed about when they first broke into the profession. "It makes it tougher on today's coaches," Falk said. "They have to teach their players to remain focused on their immediate goal and disregard all the trash that gets sent through tweets. As a coach you're teaching players how to handle those situations in order to be more successful in life after they graduate."

Falk also notices a major change in practices during the week and on Saturdays in the locker room before a game starts. "It used to be that on gamedays, all the players would show up to the locker room with the same look on their faces," Falk said. "We called it our 'gamefaces.' There was more of a unified tunnel vision about reaching their goal. Every one of them had that same game look on their face. Only whispers filled the room. Each player was zeroed in on the moment. There was no time for smiling. No time for horsing around. No time for anything but concentration on the game that kept creeping closer and closer. Now they all have their little electronic gadgets. They have earphones plugged into each ear and all are listening to the music of their choice. Nothing wrong with that, but it sure is different from what it used to be."

Another major change that Falk endured during his 40-year reign of the locker room is the direction the recruiting war has taken. "Recruiting now has become a 365-day-a-year job," Falk said. "Twenty-four/seven, and there really are no geographical boundaries."

It used to be that Michigan filled its roster primarily with players from the Midwest with states like Michigan, Ohio, Illinois, and Indiana. There were plenty of premium players to go around. With a sprinkling of big-time national recruits from places such as Florida and California, coaches like Bo and Woody Hayes had their picks of the crop.

But somewhere around the time when college football telecasts exploded on TV sets around the country, so too did the recruitment of players who had never taken a step inside the state of Michigan before. Some wanted to go to Michigan because of Bo or Mo or Lloyd or RichRod or Brady or certain members of staff assistants. Some loved the campus. Some were overwhelmed by The Big House. Some were impressed by the Tunnel. And some were flat out dazzled by the uniforms and stripes on the helmet.

Recruiting services became a year-round industry of its own. The pressure from loyalists to sign a batch of four and five-star rated recruits continues to spike each year. It's become a race for the stars. "Sometimes I wonder how the coaches can squeeze in enough time to practice during the week with such a packed recruiting schedule," Falk said.

Falk never douses the enthusiasm of the Michigan faithful pertaining to the recruiting wars. But he cautions zealots to wait until a recruit has played at least a couple of years. "The recruiting wars generate a little excitement during the offseason, but they really don't mean much until those four and five-stars do it on the field," Falk said. "When someone tells me that a certain recruit is a can't miss prospect, I tell him to come see me in three years to see just how much that player couldn't miss."

Falk played a critical role in those crucial official visit weekends when a highly regarded prospect was accompanied on campus by his parents. Falk would have a locker filled with a complete Michigan uniform—properly sized, of course—for the entire family to view. The number on the jersey would match the one the player was wearing for his high school senior year. And, of course, it was mandatory for the player to slip that winged helmet onto his head and casually walk in front of a mirror just to take a peek at how those stripes looked on his head.

In addition to having a complete uniform for each prospect, Falk spent a good portion of recruiting weekends spinning yarns about University of Michigan tradition. If a player doesn't get excited over Falk's electrifying sales pitch, nothing short of a cattle prod will get that player's attention. No school is as rich in tradition as Michigan, which has more victories than any other institution.

Falk used to talk about The Big House, college football's largest stadium. He talked about and showed each family the Little Brown Jug, college football's oldest rivalry game. He talked about the Paul Bunyan Trophy in the annual battle with Michigan State. He sang "Hail to the Victors" to get their adrenaline flowing. He introduced them to Michigan Heisman Trophy winners Charles Woodson and Desmond Howard, who sometimes just happen to be on campus for a particularly important recruiting weekend.

Falk loved to watch the faces of all the prospects who were able to take their first run through the Tunnel that leads from the Michigan locker room to the field. And the smiles on the faces of those recruits that light up the

While talking to recruits, Jon Falk emphasized the tradition behind the Paul Bunyan Trophy given to the winner of the annual game between Michigan and Michigan State.

mammoth scoreboard is one of the features from a recruiting weekend that will stick in a prospect's mind forever. As Falk spun his stories about the history of Michigan football, he paid particular attention to the mothers and fathers who have accompanied their sons on the visit. "You have to make eye contact with that mom and pop," Falk said. "They want to be assured that their boy will be taken care of during his first venture away from home."

Falk also used to stress the excellence of a Michigan education. "Michigan is the type of school that will take you to a lot of places," he used to say. "The name of Michigan will get a graduate through the door. What happens next is up to the individual. Being a former Michigan football player, though, can get someone through the tightest door."

Falk believes that one of the biggest recruiting tools is one of the smallest items in the locker room. "It's the ring," Falk said, convincingly. "Kids love to see those championship rings."

For Falk, as the most decorated staff member of Michigan football with 17 Big Ten championship rings and another handful of rings from various bowl games, there's one ring that outsparkles all the rest…at least for the moment. For Falk, it's the diamond-encrusted beauty that all players, coaches, and staff members of the Michigan team were given for winning the 2012 Sugar Bowl against Virginia Tech. In keeping with his self-made tradition of his favorite ring being his "next one," that one from the Sugar Bowl will forever be his last. "That Sugar Bowl victory came after three dismal seasons," Falk said. "It shows how much fight Michigan truly has. I'm very proud of that one."

Falk believes that of all the recruiting tools at his disposal those rings often are the deal sealers. "The kids love 'em," Falk said. "They represent all of the work and commitment it takes to win even one. Seeing those rings up close sends a message that they have a chance to win a few at Michigan, too."

Once Michigan wins its next championship, Falk is likely to remove that Sugar Bowl ring and replace it with the stunning beauty given for winning the 1997 National Championship. Michigan went undefeated and beat Washington State for the national title. Falk tells the recruits about how

Big Jon would wow recruits by showing off the extensive collection of championship rings he earned while at Michigan.

many people walking down the street stop to ask what the beautiful ring represents. "I'm always asked which one of my rings is my favorite," Falk said. "I always tell them the next one. You have got to be hungry for the next one. There are plenty of fingers just waiting for the next one."

Falk taught that lesson to quarterback Tom Brady, who has earned four Super Bowl championship rings with the New England Patriots and truly believes that the next ring will be his best ring. Falk admits he does feel special about the national championship ring and the ring he received for defeating Virginia Tech in the Sugar Bowl in 2012. Falk is convinced that there are more championship rings for Michigan to be won. And upon seeing any of the current players, Falk reminds all of them that the next ring they win will be the best one.

Chapter **11**
The Harbaugh Boys

Not so long ago, Big Jon and his wife, Cheri, were having dinner at the Delkwood Grill, an informally chic place where good food and good stories are shared, in Marietta, Georgia. As the couple enjoyed the main course, an affable young man approached the table where Falk and Cheri sat. "I recognize your face," said the smiling young man who turned out to be the owner. "I know who you are."

Falk set his memory into motion to determine who this polite young restaurateur may be. "I'm Paul Chutich," the courteous man said. "When I was a little boy, Jim Harbaugh and I used to run around in the Michigan football locker room. We used to try to get the gloves and wrist bands that Rick Leach used to wear in practice. We were big Rick Leach fans. Jim and I could pretty much beat you running around the locker room all the time. Mostly Jim. He was good at everything."

A big smile cut across Paul's face. "I remember now," Falk said. "You guys used to scoot around faster than some of our players could run."

Paul's father, Matt, owned a restaurant in Ann Arbor called Bimbo's on the Hill. It was a popular sports establishment with its Michigan leanings and loyalties hanging proudly on the walls. Bo and Big Jon sometimes feasted at the establishment.

The Harbaugh name, of course, is legendary in Ann Arbor. Father Jack was a defensive backs coach under Bo before moving to Western Michigan to become that school's head coach. Son John Harbaugh wound up as head coach of the Baltimore Ravens. He led the Ravens to victory against the San Francisco 49ers and his younger brother in Super Bowl XLVII. It's a story line made in Hollywood...except no one would believe it.

Jim, of course, was an All-American football quarterback at Michigan, a first-round draft pick selected by the Chicago Bears, a Pro Bowl quarterback for the Indianapolis Colts, head coach at San Diego and Stanford, and now head coach and living legend at the University of Michigan.

During the time the Harbaugh family came to Michigan, Falk was living alone in an apartment at the university golf course. Mama Jackie Harbaugh loved to cook, and Big Jon loved to eat with the Harbaugh boys. "I got to be real close with the family," Falk said. "Jimmy would always hang around the locker room because Rick Leach was his idol. Jim was what we used to call a gym rat. He was a sports junkie, around all the time. The bigger the challenge, the more he wanted the ball."

That was at every level—high school, college, and pros.

Falk was fortunate to have worked with a long list of sparkling quarterbacks at Michigan who went on to play in the NFL. He refuses to rate them, but their names are unforgettable to Michigan fans around the world. Guys like Tom Brady, Rick Leach, Dennis Franklin, Drew Henson, John Wangler, Steve Smith, Elvis Grbac, Michael Taylor, Brian Griese, John Navarre, Chad Henne, Denard Robinson, and Devin Gardner, just to name a few. They all tasted the top of big-time college football.

However, having known Jim since when he was a young boy, Falk knew Jim was a little different from anyone he played with or against. "Jim is what I call a stallion," Falk said. "Stallions are a little different than any other kind

As Rick Leach reaches the end zone, a young Jim Harbaugh can't wait for his shot at leading the team as a quarterback. (Courtesy the Harbaugh family)

of horse. They're strong. They're runners. They're jumpers. They dare people to look them in the eye. Don't ever try to break a stallion because they are free souls. You break a stallion, and all that's left is a pony at a carnival ride."

None of that means Harbaugh is wild. "He's just as confident and determined as Bo was," Falk said. One of the most celebrated examples that reflects that ironclad confidence occurred in 1986 when he guaranteed a victory over the vaunted Ohio State Buckeyes in the traditional final game of the season. When Falk heard about Harbaugh's guarantee, he immediately went into Bo's office and said, "Hey, did you hear what Harbaugh said?" Bo looked at Falk and said, "That's my boy."

When Jim was in high school in Palo Alto, California, he visited Miami of Ohio for a possible football scholarship. The next day Falk walked into Bo's office and said he had heard that Jimmy Harbaugh was looking at Miami. Bo put his arm around Falk and said: "Harbaugh is coming to Michigan. He just does not know it yet."

After signing Jim to a scholarship tender, Bo called Falk into his office to deliver him the good news. "Falk," Bo barked. "Get yourself prepared, Jon. Jimmy is coming to Michigan." Falk laughed and wanted to make sure about what he had just heard.

"You mean that little kid that used to hang around the locker room all the time?" Falk asked.

"That's the one," Bo said "And he's going to be a great one."

Falk worked with countless players who flashed five-star talent during his 40 years at Michigan. But Jim Harbaugh possessed a little something extra. It's the kind of talent impossible to coach into a player and just as tough to truly explain. "The first thing Jim will tell you is how much he learned from Bo," Falk said.

Falk is thrilled with the selection of Jim Harbaugh as the new Michigan head coach. Just as Harbaugh correctly guaranteed a victory over Ohio State in 1986, Falk guarantees a Michigan Big Ten championship in the not-too-distant future. "It may not be the first year, but his experience and relentlessness will make it happen soon," Falk said. "That's the way Jimmy attacks everything—playing, coaching, or even watching film from a game. Brother John is the kind of coach that prepares himself totally to give everything for victory. Jim gets himself prepared and then goes out and tells the opponent that he is going to win. And he usually does."

In 1984 Jimmy broke his arm against Michigan State in the fifth game of the season. After his arm was placed in a cast, he began hanging around the equipment room more often.

"Now that I can't play, you're the only guy that will talk to me anymore," he joked with Falk.

And the friendship between the two grew and grew. He bounced back from injury and was picked as an All-American before getting drafted by the Bears. "There are a lot of similarities between Bo and Jimmy," Falk observed. "They share a certain brand of competitiveness and determination. They never merely walk into a room…they explode into it. Both have a certain kind of presence you just can't simply teach."

Chapter *12*

Inspiring Words

I t's a distinction not found in any official record book. But without a doubt, Big Jon Falk is the runaway holder of this unofficial record. From Bo to Mo to Carr to RichRod to Hoke, Big Jon is the only man to "have heard 'em all." About 400 of them, actually. That includes pregame speeches and halftime speeches and postgame speeches. After listening to the revved-up rhetoric of so many, Falk has come to a one-word conclusion.

Overrated!

Some speeches make a point irrefutably clear. Like a root canal done on a front tooth without a generous dose of Novocain. In fact, some speeches do provide that flickering spark that just might carry an entire team through the first half of a game.

But be careful what you wish for. If someone is waiting for that fire-and-brimstone classic that almost every Hollywood football movie features, it's wiser to visit a campsite tent revival than a college locker room. Over the course of 40 years, Falk has heard all the words of pleas, praises, challenges, and outright threats to fill all the space in *The American Heritage Dictionary*.

"Speeches are fine if the speaker has something really good to say," Falk said. "But what he says better be real good because no amount of words are strong enough to overcome a clearly superior opponent. And the speech better be fresh, not just a bag of words that some members of the team have heard four years in a row. You don't want to eat a head of lettuce that was picked a couple of months ago."

Falk is convinced that continual technological advances in communication have evened the playing field quite a lot for many of the schools in most conferences. It's tough to top that type of technological efficiency, even with a bagful of imploring words. "With all of those technological changes like the Internet, blogs, twitters, and tweets, teams have up-to-the moment information on every opponent," Falk said. "We know how to beat them, and they know how to beat us. That's not to say outcomes are determined even before the teams take the field. But a whole truckload of words isn't going to change how a team plays unless execution of the game plan is followed."

And that doesn't always happen.

Falk, though, does believe the charisma and demeanor of a coach certainly can help a player perform up to his ability—sometimes a rung or two above.

Bo was a master in drama. He knew how to blend his God-given charisma with a game plan that varied little from one week to the next. "Bo could coax a turtle into running a 4.4 second 40," Falk said. "That's how strong his will and spirits were. If there wasn't time enough to go around a wall, he'd have his players go right through it. A wall only hurts for a moment. The remnants of one of Bo's tirades could last for a couple of plays."

Bo also just happened to carry a special weapon in his back pocket that could whip three or four pockets full of words. "He could cry in the blink of an eye," Falk said. "It was amazing. He could turn it on and off like a light switch. Never saw anything like it. Those tears were real and almost always got the job done. For special games by the time Bo finished one of his pre-game speeches, a whole locker room full of players was red-eyed and ready to whip anyone who dared to step in the way."

One of Bo's most stirring speech performances occurred in 1975 on the Friday evening before the game against Northwestern. All the Michigan players were in their rooms at the team hotel in Ann Arbor when suddenly Bo was struck with the notion that the Wildcats were only a few hours away from what would have been the upset of the entire college football schedule.

Bo scampered to each player's room with a spontaneous early pregame message. "I want you guys to know that if we don't play our best game tomorrow, Northwestern is going to beat us," he told everyone. "They're hungry. I can feel it. You've got to play your best game. You've got to take it to them, or we are going to get beat. Now go back to sleep and get yourself ready."

Bo always had a gift for being able to inspire everyone to play just a little bit better than even the player realized he could, Falk said. On that Saturday after Bo's ominous plea, Michigan showed it came to play. "No one said a word in the locker room before the game," Falk said. "They took Bo's late-night warning seriously. There was no laughing, no joking. I could tell when we came through the Tunnel that Northwestern was in for a long day."

The Michigan players obviously had taken Bo's Friday night words to heart. The final score was Michigan 69, Northwestern 0.

A simple but stirring halftime performance by Lloyd Carr in 2003 is one Falk will always remember. Playing at the Metrodome in Minnesota, the Golden Gophers jumped to a 14–0 lead.

In the locker room during halftime, Carr gathered the team around him and methodically challenged every person in the room. "You're going to let this happen to Michigan?" Carr said, sounding like Bo—or perhaps George Scott in the movie *Patton*.

He looked around the room, peering from one set of eyes to another. Then he proceeded to walk around the room, challenging each individual to know what he was going to do throughout the second half. "Well, I'm not going to let that happen," Carr said with a piercing conviction. "This is Michigan. I will not let this happen."

Even after hearing hundreds of halftime speeches, Falk said there was

Coach Lloyd Carr, an extremely well-read individual, took a cerebral approach with his pregame speeches.

something inexplicably different in Carr's challenge that time. "I can't explain it, but something special happened," Falk said. "Those boys would have walked the plank over a school of sharks for Lloyd that night."

Michigan rallied back in the second half for a 38–35 victory. "Sounds simple and almost make-believe, but it was one of the best speeches and coaching jobs I had ever seen," Falk said.

Carr was never a shouter like Bo was. He was more cerebral in his approach to coaching and preparing his teams. He was a prolific reader and used his literary discoveries to motivate his teams. Throughout the national championship season of 1997, Carr used author Jon Krakauer's nonfiction best-seller *Into Thin Air* to motivate his team through its unbeaten season. It's the story about taming the perils of climbing Mount Everest on a rescue mission. As the rescue team ascended higher, the risks to reach the top became more perilous.

Carr knew he had a special team, one that was prepared for the risks and dangers of challenging for the national title. With each successive victory, he used metaphors from the book. There was no room for mistakes. "We're getting there," he cautioned his team each week. "But the air is getting thinner, and we aren't there yet."

Finally, before the Ohio State showdown, Carr informed his team it was ready to play for the Big Ten championship. They had survived all the challenges and turned all doubts into a Big Ten championship. It was onto the national title game against Washington State in the Rose Bowl. "I'll never forget standing in that locker room after that game in the Rose Bowl," Falk said. "When Coach Carr announced to his team that it had just won the national title, tears streamed down the cheeks of almost every person in that room. Cheers in the locker room from Pasadena boomed all the way down to Tijuana."

Falk's eyes still get a little damp just thinking about that entire season. "Lloyd had developed one of the most effective motivational programs for an entire season," Falk said. "He didn't have to deliver any fire-and-brimstone speech. He had the whole season charted, and it worked."

Some of the most effective and memorable speeches spontaneously arise out of the players themselves. In the 1997 game against Iowa at The Big House, the Hawkeyes took a 21–7 lead into halftime looking to derail Michigan's undefeated string. "Your undefeated season is coming to an unscheduled stop," the Hawkeyes were screaming at the Michigan players as both teams jostled through the Tunnel for halftime. "It's over today Michigan. You're goin' down…You're goin' down."

The locker room was basically quiet until quarterback Brian Griese walked to the middle of the room. "Listen up, men," the fifth-year senior said in a level but stirring tone of voice.

He told the team that he had just played the worst half of his entire career. "But I guarantee you one thing," Griese continued. "I'm going out there to play the best second half of my life. I want you to join me. I promise you that the only winner walking out of this stadium today is going to be wearing maize and blue."

It wasn't merely the words Griese used to get his message across. It was the spirit and confidence that he gave to the rest of the players. "I knew when I heard him talk that we were going to win that day," Falk said. "No doubt in my mind that little talk by Griese gave us the little mental shove over the top."

The final score was Michigan 28, Iowa 24.

Quarterback Jim Harbaugh was a gifted speaker, Falk said. He had a natural gift for leadership. "He was basically a rah-rah guy," Falk said. "He had enough confidence boiling inside his belly that he could spare a little shot of adrenaline to the rest of the team. He'd go around the locker room and say a few words to everyone. He promised them that he was going to play a great game and he just tried to share that feeling with them. Jon Jansen was the same character like that in a lot of ways."

One of Falk's favorite players was running back Rob Lytle. "He had so much guts and absolutely no fear in his belly," Falk said. "He also was one of the most unselfish players I ever was around."

Lytle uncharacteristically fumbled away the ball three times in the 16–14 upset loss to Purdue in 1976. It put Michigan into the perilous position of having to defeat Illinois and Ohio State to make it to the Rose Bowl.

In the subdued Michigan locker room after the loss to Purdue, Lytle called the team around him and promised them they would never see him fumble the ball away like that ever again. On Sunday before the team meeting, Falk taped a handle to a football and placed it inside of Lytle's locker. Upon discovering the taped ball, Lytle walked into the equipment room and asked who had placed the ball there.

Falk knew Lytle well and was certain he would meet the challenge. He told Lytle Michigan could not afford such miscues in the next two games. "Take the handle off, Jon," he said to Falk. "No one could use a jackhammer to get that ball away from me the rest of the way."

Michigan then went on to defeat Illinois and Ohio State for a trip to the Rose Bowl. "The speeches are not like they look in the movies," Falk said. "But the real leaders somehow get their message across. That's what true leaders do. It's not about the words they use. It's more about the emotions in head and heart that fire up a team to play to the level of its talent. That's all any coach really wants his team to do—play up to the talent level of each player on the team. Michigan always has been blessed with talent and the means to share it throughout the team. That's far more rewarding than any speech in a movie."

Chapter 13
Bo Changes

I t was perhaps hard to believe and noticeable only to Jon Falk, but there was a change in Bo at Michigan. Believe it or not, Bo had become more docile (as crazy as that sounds) than when he coached at Miami of Ohio. "Bo was a lot more volatile at Miami," Falk said.

The difference was subtle—something like measuring the difference of getting wetter in Lake Superior than in a backyard swimming pool. But it was apparent to Falk. And Falk was excited about getting ready to work for Bo.

Bo was still incurably passionate about football, his job, his team, and how he attacked each aspect of life. He had simply enhanced all of his talents, which resulted in a confidence truly unshakable. "Bo had become an excellent teacher," Falk said. "He would chew you out if you made a mistake. Then he'd take the time to explain what you did wrong and how he wanted something executed. When the incident was over, it was forgotten. You just better remember not to make the same mistake again."

Falk was fired several times for some flimsy reason or another just because Bo needed to vent. He always rehired him the very next day. "Bo would 'fire' someone almost every day," Falk said, "sometimes even more. Then he would rehire the person before practice was over. That was just Bo. He knew how he wanted things to be done and was upfront with all the people he led. You never had to wonder about what Bo wanted. That's the sign of a great leader."

The subtle change in Bo was reflected in the command he had established over the storied program of Michigan football. "Whenever there's a coaching change, it takes a while for the new staff to establish the program they want to run," Falk explained. "Once they do, it becomes their program and then it's a matter of maintaining that standard."

Bo did it in lightning speed with the stunning upset of No. 1 ranked Ohio State in the final game of the 1969 season. From that day forward, it was Bo's program. He was able to shape his players—present and future—along with his staff and the Michigan alumni into a program fully vested in Bo. "No one ever knows for sure how even one season will finish, but I have a gut feeling that Jimmy Harbaugh is going to be a lot like Bo," Falk said.

The fire inside Bo was as scorching as it had been while he coached at Miami. Falk witnessed Bo's passion at Michigan and it was obvious to him that Bo had grown. As the 1974 season approached, Falk was receiving his own cram course in all of the traditions that live nowhere else but Michigan. When he first came to Ann Arbor, he knew only two things. He knew that Bo Schembechler was the head coach. And he knew that almost everyone in Ohio hates Michigan.

Two of the most celebrated traditions infused into all new players and members of the football staff are the marching band and the mystique of the Tunnel. On gamedays the two distinctively singular entities combine to create an almost surreal experience for any coach, player, or staff member who takes a step onto that field. "A lot of people don't know how much Bo loved that band," Falk said. "He felt it was an essential part of every Saturday. He actually used it to our advantage."

Organized with nearly 30 members in 1896, the Michigan Marching Band now features 235 members and is one of the most celebrated units in modern college football. As with all incoming freshman players and new staff members, Falk had to learn the lyrics and melody to "The Victors" long before the first kickoff of the season. Short, rousing, and loaded with the impact of a jackhammer, "The Victors" is the most celebrated college fight song in America.

Written by Louis Elbel in 1898 following a Michigan upset of the powerful University of Chicago coached by the legendary Amos Alonzo Staff, "The Victors" has withstood every test of time. "The Victors" is played when the band takes the field after exiting the Tunnel. It is raucously sung by the team in the locker room after each victory. Legendary band director Dr. William Revelli taught each freshman player to sing the song with as much vigor as he performed it. And each player, coach, and staff member better know every word and note long before the season starts. "Bo would set up special times after practice for the band to come over and play for us," Falk said. "Sometimes during breaks of two-a-day practices, we were made to stand up and sing 'The Victors.'"

Another familiar favorite played constantly each Saturday is the "Let's Go Blue" chant. And that's where the Tunnel provides a stimulating special effect that almost feels spooky. The Tunnel is a 300-foot gauntlet leading from the locker rooms to the field. For both teams there's only one way out to the field and one way back.

When the team is returning to the locker room after completing its pregame warm-ups, the band congregates at the back of the Tunnel and begins to play "Let's Go Blue." "When the players are running up that tunnel and hear that music, you can see their feet almost floating above the ground," Falk said. "There's a lot of bumping and grinding going on, and you can just feel all the excitement building up."

Once inside the locker room, the team can still hear the band playing before taking the field. "When you hear all that and feel all that, every player in the room knows he's into something bigger than he ever dreamed," Falk said.

No one forgets his first trip down the Tunnel, and that swirling rush of adrenaline stays with each individual for the rest of his life. The late Michigan All-American and All-Pro tight end Ron Kramer shivered at the feeling. "The first time I did it, I thought I was going to pee in my pants," Kramer said. "There's no feeling like that tunnel anywhere else in sports. It's impossible to put into words."

Dan Dierdorf, a Michigan All-American tackle and member of the Pro Football Hall of Fame, treasured every trip through the Tunnel. "One minute you're in darkness, and the next you're in the middle of 110,000 screaming people," he said. "It seems like the whole world is watching."

When both teams get tangled in the Tunnel at the end of the first half or after the game, the trash talk, the taunting, and "accidental" elbows to the ribs turn into a game itself. Through the years, Michigan has used the mystique of the Tunnel for even the slightest advantage before the first kick.

Falk's first trip down the Tunnel came during the season opener against Iowa in 1974. He was only 23 years old and probably more nervous than the players around him. "Like all the players, I remember jumping up and touching the Go Blue banner that the Varsity M club holds at the center of the field," Falk said. "I'm a little too old to get up that high now, but I still loved running across the field and touching the banner with my hat."

Falk also got his first experience of singing "The Victors" in the locker room after that first Iowa game. Michigan jumped to a 14–0 first-quarter lead and finished with a 24–7 victory.

The following week Colorado came to The Big House for a nationally tele-vised game with Keith Jackson calling the play-by-play. Bill Mallory, whom Falk worked with and succeeded Bo at Miami of Ohio, was the head coach for Colorado. Milan Vooletich, who had lived next door to the Falk home in Oxford, Ohio, was one of his assistants. During the Colorado walk-through of the field on Friday, Falk led his former coaches through the Tunnel onto the field. "This isn't that impressive," Falk remembers Vooletich saying.

Jackson, a veteran who had broadcast countless memorable games at

The Big House, was following the visiting coaches a few steps behind and smiled. "Just wait 'til tomorrow," he promised in his trademark dramatic drawl. "Just wait 'til tomorrow."

Colorado got the message loud and clear as Michigan scored in each quarter in a relatively easy 31–0 rout. Falk was getting a taste for another Michigan tradition. The Wolverines had notched four shutouts during their 10-game winning streak leading up to the traditional season-ending classic with Ohio State in Columbus.

Every day of the season served as preparation for the Ohio State game. Bo had a schedule on the wall of the team meeting room. At Sunday meetings he finished his message to the team by analyzing how it had progressed during the prior week. He would talk about the upcoming game. Then he'd finish his weekly assessment by pointing to the last game on the schedule. "Men, we're not good enough," he'd say. "Not good enough to play this team down here. We must play better. We must work harder."

The week before the Ohio State showdown, Michigan exploded for a 51–0 whipping of Purdue. "Men, we are now ready," he began his Sunday session. "We are now ready for Ohio State. We are primed. We are ready."

This was Falk's first trip to the Horseshoe, and it left an indelible imprint on his mind. "My whole life I had dreamed about going to the Rose Bowl," Falk said. "I thought there was no other thing bigger in sports than the Rose Bowl. Coming from Ohio, of course, I always followed Ohio State and Woody Hayes. But I was true blue Michigan now. And we had a chance at going to the Rose Bowl with one more victory."

Bo was still chaffing over the 1973 game in Ann Arbor that ended in the classic 10–10 tie. Both teams finished with 10–0–1 records, but a vote by Big Ten Conference athletic directors gave the Rose Bowl berth to Ohio State.

At Columbus, the Wolverines indeed looked as if they were good enough by jumping to a 10–0 lead in the first quarter. The defense was impenetrable the entire game. Only once did the Buckeyes get inside Michigan's 25-yard line. But that drive resulted in a 35-yard field goal to lift Ohio State to a

12–10 victory and another Rose Bowl bid. Each team grounded out 195 rushing yards, but Michigan outgained Ohio State 96–58 in the air.

The loss meant that the 1972–74 Michigan teams had lost only two games and tied one. And none of those players had gone to a bowl game. The situation only infuriated Bo more as he continued his drive to open up the Big Ten to more bowl bids. It was later that year that the conference ruled in favor of any Big Ten team to play in a bowl to which it was invited. "Every conference team should get down on their knees and thank Bo for what he did," Falk said. "That opened the door for all the bowl games we have today."

Chapter **14**
Home Sweet Home

Looking back at his 40 years at Michigan, Big Jon can laugh at some of the peculiarities of different situations. The transition from Miami of Ohio to the big stage of Michigan was exciting for Falk. His new team had precision drills and razor sharp intensity, but plenty of laughs along the way.

Falk also realized the opportunity he'd been given at Michigan. He was working for one of the most dynamic young coaches in the game. He felt privileged to be at one of America's leading academic universities. And he had a new home just off the 18th green of the prestigious University of Michigan Golf Course. It was right across the street from The Big House and a convenient walk to the football offices and practice facilities.

Well, the place wasn't really new. And it wasn't actually a home. It was a three-room first-floor apartment at the corner of the building that housed the pro shop, a string of offices, and meeting rooms. The second floor featured a long row of empty offices that were converted into rooms for various athletes on athletic scholarships.

Falk's one-bedroom apartment featured a kitchen with just enough space for a designated living area. A full bathroom provided all the comforts of home. Never to be mistaken for being plush, the apartment was comfortable and convenient enough for Falk to spend his first 15 years in Ann Arbor there. The apartment had one particularly attractive feature. With athletic director Don Canham having designated Falk as the unofficial "guardian" of the golf course once everyone had left the facility for the day, it came totally rent free.

When Falk's mother Jean, grandmother Rosella Land, and uncle Don Falk drove up from Oxford to visit him for the first time that spring, the family approved of the living conditions except for one matter. Mama Falk addressed the issue with Bo. "Coach Schembechler," she said, "I know you have a lot of power around here. Can you please get those big trash cans outside my son's back door cleaned?"

In his entire coaching career, that was the first time Bo had ever been asked to resolve a custodial situation. "Yeah...ol' Bo is gonna work on getting those cans real clean," he said with a laugh.

Falk quickly discovered a variety of benefits from living on campus. When Bo or any of the assistant coaches were on the road recruiting, Falk was usually invited to one of the coaches' homes for dinner. "I used to go over to Bo's house maybe two or three times a week to eat dinner with Millie and the boys," Falk said. "When Bo came home, we'd sit around in the living room watching TV or listen to Bo about who he was recruiting."

Living in the apartment provided Falk with other experiences, such as getting close to new assistant coaches when they were hired. "Bo would call me up and tell me to take them in for a little while until they got situated," Falk said.

Lloyd Carr spent time in the apartment when he was hired as an assistant. So did Don Nehlen, who moved on to West Virginia as the head coach. He later hired Rich Rodriguez as one of his assistants. Paul Schudel and Milan Voolitich's family also were treated to Jon's friendly confines at the golf course.

Not too many people receive an overnight visit from a former president (Gerald Ford) at their apartment on the university golf course. But Big Jon did.

Falk got booted from his apartment for a couple of days in 1976 when a former Michigan player happened to be in town to participate in a charity golf tournament. "Now Jon," Bo told him, "President [Gerald] Ford is coming to town. We need a place for him to relax near the golf course during the day. We're gonna have him stay at your place."

Needless to say, Falk was surprised.

"Coach Schembechler, what am I supposed to do?" he asked.

Bo looked back as if the question was simple enough for any second grader. "You're going to move out," he said.

Simple as that, the matter was settled.

For two weeks leading up to the tournament, Bo asked if the apartment was clean. Falk assured him positively each time. "The president is coming," Bo would say. "That's the president of the United States of America. He's staying in your apartment, Jon. I want that place cleaner than the Board of Health."

Bo must have felt anxious about the situation because he sent his secretary, Lynn Koch, to inspect the apartment. Upon her report, Bo's message to Falk was simple and clear. "You're getting out early," Bo informed Falk. "We're sending in a professional cleaner."

Falk had to visit his apartment shortly after the president arrived. After clearing himself with the Secret Service agents, he walked into the living room that, for the moment, belonged to the most powerful man on the planet. Falk discovered the president sitting on the couch smoking his pipe and reading a book. "Mr. President," Falk said. "My name is Jon Falk, and I'm proud to have you use my apartment."

The president reached out to shake Falk's hand. He smiled and said that Bo had told him a lot of nice things about Falk. "I just have to ask you one favor, sir," Falk said. "If you play golf with Bo today, will you please tell him that the place is clean? He's been on me for the last two weeks to have it sparkling for you."

The president scanned the rooms and nodded his approval. "The place looks fine, Jon," he said. "Everything here looks fine. It's a great place for me to rest during the day."

Falk thanked the president, and the two shared a few words about the Michigan football team that the president had once played for. "If you ever come to town again and need a place to stay, you're always welcome here, Mr. President," Falk finished.

The president graciously smiled. "Well if I do, Jon. I'll give you two weeks' notice, so you can get it cleaned up for me," he cracked.

Seasons slipped by quickly for Falk, who spent his first 15 years in that apartment. He then purchased his first home in Ann Arbor and began to date his eventual wife, Cheri Boychuck-Winkle. A year later, Bo made the appropriate wedding toast. Now the last staff member who comprised "Bo's Boys," Falk has obviously made his own imprint on the most tradition-rich college football program in the country.

Chapter **15**

In the Face of Woody Hayes

O n the day before the 1975 season finale against Ohio State, Jon Falk
got his first in-your-face encounter with the man he had so admired
as a youngster—Woody Hayes. It was cold and snowy that Friday afternoon when the Buckeyes' bus pulled up to the stadium for practice. Bo had
instructed Falk and associate athletic director Don Lund to inform the legendary coach that the tarp was on the field, and there would be no practice.
"Coach Hayes rolled his jaw about three times," Falk said. "Then he took his
index finger and stuck it into my left shoulder blade. It still hurts today."

"Every time I come to Michigan, all they want to do is screw me…screw
me," Hayes growled.

"Yes sir, Coach Hayes, but you still can't practice because the tarp is on
the field," Falk persisted.

Hayes proceeded down the Tunnel and managed to talk the groundskee-
pers into removing the tarp from half the field. Falk immediately returned to
Bo's office to tell him the Buckeyes were practicing.

"Where?" Bo demanded.

"In the stadium," Falk replied.

Bo shook his head and couldn't hide a smile.

"The old man doesn't miss a trick, does he?" Bo said. "He doesn't miss a trick."

Before Saturday's game, Bo instructed Falk to go to the visitors' locker room and tell Coach Hayes to take the field first. Upon the first knock, the door opened, and there stood Woody staring straight into Falk's eyes.

"Sir, Coach Schembechler asked for you to take the field first," Falk said.

Woody said nothing. A few tense moments later, he slammed the door shut in pure Woody fashion that almost cost Falk a finger in the door. Falk told Bo, who again ordered him to deliver the message. Again Woody opened the door and once more slammed it shut.

Three minutes later with Falk still standing in the Tunnel, Woody opened the door and led his team out without saying a word. "Coach Hayes was an intense guy," Falk said. "When I came to Michigan, Coach Schembechler told me, 'Whenever we play Ohio State, take care of them. Give them whatever they need. We want to beat them, but we respect them. Whatever they want, you better take care of it. And take care of Coach Hayes.'"

As he did before all Ohio State games, Falk toured the locker room, reminding all players that they would never experience more fierce hitting than what they were about to face. Rick Leach was getting the first of his four shots as the starting quarterback against the Buckeyes. Before the kickoff Falk grabbed Leach's face mask and told him to "tighten it up." Leach liked it a little more loose because it made it easier to call audibles at the line.

On the first play, Leach rolled left on the option and precisely pitched the ball to a trailing back. The defender assigned to Leach was indifferent to the pitch. His job was simple—finish the play by knocking the quarterback into Monday morning.

Before the next possession, Leach visited Falk to have his chinstrap tightened.

Michigan limited two-time Heisman Trophy winner Archie Griffin to

46 yards. The Wolverines held a 14–7 lead with five minutes to play when a critical third-and-15 pass was completed to Brian Baschnagel to keep the game-tying drive alive. Ohio State scored again to win 21–14.

Years later, Falk was visited by a sports equipment sales representative who introduced himself as Brian Baschnagel. In the middle of their conversation, Falk put the name and face together. "Hey," Falk shouted. "You're the S.O.B. who caught that third-and-15 pass back in '75."

As the pair reminisced, the late, celebrated Michigan radio broadcaster Bob Ufer entered the locker room. It didn't take him long to recognize Falk's visitor. "You're the S.O.B. who caught that third-and-15 back in '75," Ufer said.

Now all three were laughing and sharing old Bo and Woody stories. When it was time for Baschnagel to leave, he shook hands with both men. "You know, Brian," Falk said. "You would have made a great 'Michigan Man.'"

Chapter **16**

A.C.

In 1979 a kid from Rivera Beach, Florida, came to Michigan. When Bo and Big Jon were going over the numbers for that fall, Bo said they were going to give Anthony Carter uniform No.1, which is normally given to the best wide receiver on the team. Bo looked at Falk and said Anthony Carter would be the most exciting player to come to Michigan in a long time.

"He will become the Johnny Rodgers of college football," he said. Johnny Rodgers played for Nebraska and won the Heisman trophy in 1972. Rodgers became known as "the Jet." Carter became known as "the Snake."

Both were filled with extraordinary football talent. And in the summer of 1979 during preseason practice, it was easy to see the speed, toughness, and acrobatic skills that Carter possessed.

A.C. was known for being very shy. When someone talked to him, he had a hard time looking that person in the eye. "Anthony, don't be afraid of me," Falk said to him. "I'm your friend. From now on when I talk to you, you look at me in the face. He looked at me, smiled, and said, 'Okay, Big Jon.'"

All-American bookends—wide receiver Anthony Carter (far left) and quarterback Rick Leach (far right)—pose with Jon and Cheri Falk.

Members of the Michigan football team were hired in the summer by the athletic department to do odd jobs around the football building. During one summer, quarterback John Wangler was head of the paint patrol to upgrade the football locker room. Before having to run an errand with Wangler, Falk ordered A.C. to paint the restroom in the building. Before Falk returned with Wangler, A.C. had painted the *whole* restroom. He had painted the walls, the mirror, the sink, the toilets, the urinals, and the floors. If there had been any balls of lint hiding in a corner, they got a splash of paint, too.

When Falk and Wangler returned, the room looked hospital white. Falk told the foreman of the paint team—Wangler—that he better start fixing it and removing the extra paint so that it looked perfect before Bo showed up. "Bo comes down here at 5:00 every afternoon for a brief inspection," Falk told Wangler. When he arrived that day, he saw the paint team scraping all the paint from the tiles, mirrors, and urinals.

Bo looked at Falk and said, "What the hell happened here Falk?" Falk took responsibility for the mishap. "I told Anthony to paint the restroom, and he went out and painted every inch," Falk said. "He may have been a little too ambitious."

Bo yelled at Falk and said football started in three weeks. He told Falk he wanted the room to look like new. Bo had the paint patrol stand up at the team's first meeting. "I want to thank these young men for their hard work this summer in making sure this football building is nice. Now let's keep it that way," he said.

Falk sat in the back of the room and cracked a couple of nervous smiles.

In his last year in 2013, Falk walked out of the stadium locker room door after the first game, and there was big Ed Muransky, an offensive lineman. "He looked at me and said, 'Big Jon, you're retiring?'" Then he started to cry. "'Who am I going to come back to see? Who am I going to visit here?'"

Muransky said he and Jon would always be friends and then presented a memorable retirement gift to Falk. "That's the kind of guy Big Ed always was," Falk said.

"I want to thank you for how you treated me and my family during my time at Michigan," Muransky said. "I will always remember you and so will this university."

Falk will be remembered by all the players who turned into friends. And there are plenty. The Mallory family has longtime roots with Falk. When he was working at Miami of Ohio, Bill Mallory was the coach there. Coach Mallory and his wife, Ellie, had three young sons—Doug, Mike, and Curt. Coach Mallory came into the equipment room one day and brought three little boys with him. He said they were playing little league football and needed facemasks to protect their noses. So Falk put facemasks on the helmets of these three pepper pots who happened to have a lot of talent.

Years later, the Mallory boys would be playing for Michigan and Falk again would be putting facemasks on their helmets.

Mike and Doug also worked for Falk during the summer in the football building. One day their mother, Ellie, stopped by and wanted to make sure that Falk was taking care of her boys during that summer. He assured her that he was, and she said, "You'd better, Jon, cuz I'll come back and get you if you don't…You took care of these little boys when they were back in Oxford, Ohio, and I expect you to treat them the same here at Michigan while they are growing to be men."

Chapter 17
Curtis Greer

From his distinguished Michigan career, Curtis Greer learned that trust is earned, not merely given. That's why the former All-American defensive lineman, who spent eight years in the NFL, felt confident having his undergraduate son, Brandon, work for Jon Falk as a student assistant equipment manager. "I say thank you to Jon Falk," Curtis Greer said. "I don't know how Michigan football survives without Big Jon. He's just like Bo—honest and oozing with integrity. Both taught me how to do things the right way—the Michigan way. You can coach your kids, but others raise them. I knew Jon would teach him the right things in life that you can't find in the textbooks."

Of course, Brandon did fairly well with the books, too. After graduating from Michigan's College of Business, he earned a law degree from Michigan. He had Jon's support all the way. "Jon helped, and I thank him," Curtis Greer said.

A graduate of Cass Tech High School in Detroit, Curtis Greer and teammates Harlan Huckleby and Tom Seabron were part of the fabulous 1975 recruiting class that also featured Rick Leach, Russell Davis, and Jerry Meter. The following year Cass Tech's Roosevelt Smith joined the Michigan family. All learned quickly that Falk was a man they could trust. "Jon Falk isn't just the equipment manager," Greer said. "I view him as the vice president of operations for Michigan football for 40 years. Nothing gets done 'til John Falk gets it going. No practice. No uniforms. No balls. No buses. Nothing. He makes everything happen."

What he does behind the scenes, however, is what separates Falk from a mere job description. As a freshman, Greer observed upperclassmen such as Calvin O'Neal, Greg Morton, and Tim Davis. He watched how they acted—on the field and in the locker room. He noticed the relationship they had with Falk. He felt the admiration they felt for Falk.

Greer came to the conclusion that Falk was "one of the most integral ingredients to our success." "He's a conduit between the coaches and players," Greer said. "In good times and tough times, a player could go into his office just to get things of his chest. We talked about school. We talked about football. We talked about family. We talked about Bo. If we were bitching, he'd listen."

And when a player was finished, Falk always asked the same question—now what are you going to do about it? "That's the way he is," Greer said. "Bitching is all right to clear your mind. But it doesn't solve any problem. How you tackle a situation is what matters. Big Jon helped you find the strength to do something about it."

Greer particularly appreciated Falk's honesty even when his message wasn't exactly what a player wanted to hear. "That's why everybody admired him," Greer said. "He never worried if a player didn't like to hear what he was saying. It was always the truth. He was never a yeller. But he always got his point across. I remember him saying so many times to a player: 'Son, don't screw this up.' Jon Falk touched all of us. Besides Bo, he was the only one who touched all of us. He was an integral part of all the success we enjoyed."

Chapter **18**

John Wangler

John Wangler made Jon Falk the ultimate offer he couldn't refuse. And after Wangler delivered, Falk delivered, too. Michigan was practicing for its sixth Rose Bowl under Bo, whose teams had dropped their first five appearances. After the team arrived in California to prepare for the 1981 classic, Wangler set the stakes. "I told Jon if we beat Washington, I want my helmet and jersey," the fifth-year senior quarterback said. "I want to keep them forever."

Despite starving for that first Rose Bowl victory, Falk told him that according to the rules, he couldn't technically give them to him. Perhaps, however, something could be arranged. Under the direction of Wangler, Michigan defeated Washington 23–6. After the win he sought that famous Michigan uniform, and Falk managed to "arrange" for those memorable souvenirs to arrive safely at his Royal Oak, Michigan, home. "I wanted that helmet and jersey real bad," Wangler said. "I have them displayed in my home today, along with various other pieces of memorabilia."

Quarterback John Wangler eludes a Washington defender during Michigan's Rose Bowl victory. (Courtesy University of Michigan Athletic Department)

Wangler, of course, carved his name into Michigan folklore by tossing a pass to Anthony Carter, who zigzagged down the field to score the winning touchdown that nipped Indiana 27–21 with no time remaining in 1979. But the quarterback's gutsy play throughout his career was even more impressive. After suffering a serious knee injury midway through the second quarter of the Gator Bowl the previous season, Wangler underwent surgery and had to endure painful rehabilitation in order to be ready for the 1980 season. "Nobody rehabbed as hard as John Wangler," Falk said. "Other guys may have worked just as hard, but no one surpassed him. He was full of guts…full of determination. He promised himself he would be back."

As always, Wangler credited the coaches, his teammates, and all the devoted people at Michigan. "Jon Falk is definitely one of them," Wangler said. "Big Jon is a legend. He's one of a kind."

Wangler should know. He spent five years as a player, three as a graduate assistant under Bo, and also one summer as a worker under Falk. Along with a handful of other players, Wangler spent the summer before his final season sorting equipment, painting the football building, and anything else Falk could cook up. "Mel Owens and I were the supervisors," Wangler said. "Anthony Carter and a couple of other players worked under us."

Wangler came to appreciate Falk's offbeat humor and peculiarities. "I really came to appreciate him during my fifth year," Wangler said. "He was always charged up, always unflappable. He has this passion for Michigan football. He told us more stories about players and games and traditions that only he can remember."

During his final season as leader of the team, Wangler found himself spending more time with Falk in his office. "The beautiful thing about Jon was how you could talk to him," Wangler said. "Sometimes it's hard for a player to talk to a coach. Jon made it easy to get things off our chests. Sometimes coaches would be yelling and screaming. Jon would lend a calming effect."

Wangler also appreciated the link that Falk provided from Bo to all subsequent coaches. "Jon was like a security blanket," Wangler said. "You always knew you could go back to Ann Arbor and share old stories. He made it feel like home...like you're still part of the program. That's a feeling that will never grow old."

Wangler recalls those Fridays before games when Falk played the classic Bob Ufer tapes with the highlights of Michigan football. "He had those tapes blaring," Wangler said. "You could hear them throughout the whole building, probably all the way down to the student union building. It was one of his ways to pass along all the legacies that are so important to the program."

The quarterback even likened the longtime equipment manager to the legendary Michigan football coach. "Like Bo, Big Jon was bigger than life for me," Wangler said. "Both were great in everything they did. One critical trait they shared was that they never simply handed something to anyone. They made you work for it."

Wangler appreciated all the extra time Falk spent with him merely to help him through some tight situations. "Big Jon was an equipment manager first," Wangler said. "But he was far more than that. He was a coach...a friend...a confidante...a counselor. He'd spend the time and try to help the team be successful in any way he could. It's hard to imagine Michigan football without him...No matter what's going on with the team, you can go back to Ann Arbor and share old stories. I always feel like I'm at home with Jon."

Like all former players returning to Ann Arbor, Wangler still tries to see if Falk happens to be there. "With Jon around, you always got the feeling that all the dots would be connected," Wangler said. "That's a great sense of security. There will never be another Jon Falk."

Chapter **19**
Woody Passed the Ball

Like all great coaches, Bo never counted a victory until the clock quit ticking. Once in a while, though, there was a stunning exception. And when that opportunity arose against Ohio State, Bo squeezed it like a fresh lemon.

With a Rose Bowl bid on the line, the 1976 Michigan-Ohio State in Columbus started with a bizarre incident even before the team boarded the bus for the game. The water at the hotel where the Michigan team was staying had been "mysteriously" turned off early Saturday morning. So the players couldn't even take showers or brush their teeth. Even the toilets didn't work.

Bo and everyone connected to the team took the matter personally. "Hey, if that's the way they want to play this game, then that's the way we'll play it," Bo said. "Dirty, mean, and ornery all day long. There'll be plenty of fresh water in Pasadena when we get there."

"Every time we go to Columbus, something screwy happens," Jon Falk said. "You never know what to expect."

Perhaps even more unexpected than the convenient drought at the hotel was the final play of the first half. Bo seized the opportunity and magnified its significance to his team. The game was scoreless and crammed with the clean, bone-rattling ferocity featured in every Michigan-Ohio State game. Both defenses were viciously precise as the time ticked down in the first half. With only moments left, Ohio State mounted a drive that took the ball inside the Michigan 30-yard line. With time for one last play, Woody Hayes spurned a long field-goal attempt. Instead, the Buckeyes attempted a desperation pass into the end zone that defensive back Jim Pickens intercepted as time expired. Michigan had stopped Ohio State's best drive and would receive the second-half kickoff. "The feeling was unbelievable as we ran off the field," Falk said. "Every Michigan player suddenly felt six inches taller."

Inside the locker room, the players were hooting and hollering like sailors coming home from six months at sea. They didn't need to rest at the half. They couldn't wait to get back on the field. Amid the euphoria Bo took the floor. "Men, gather around me," he shouted. "I want you to know something right now. It' over. It's over. It's gonna be Michigan today. It's gonna be Michigan!"

Time seemed to stand still as the players waited for Bo's final declaration. "Because we just made Woody pass the football!" Bo shouted.

Again the players exploded with cheers heard probably all the way to Cleveland. "The confidence and emotion that Bo showed at the half just instilled those players with even more confidence in themselves," Falk said. "Bo could read a team. He knew what they were feeling and always had the right words for every situation. He wasn't going to let this opportunity slip away."

The second half was yet to unfold, but everyone in that room was convinced the game was waiting to be taken. And no one had to wait long. Michigan took the second-half kickoff and launched an 80-yard scoring drive with surgical precision. Later in the period, Michigan put together a 52-yard scoring drive. To make it harder for Ohio State to tie the game— a result that would've sent the Buckeyes to the Rose Bowl—Michigan eschewed an extra-point, and instead holder Jerry Zuver sprang to his feet and raced around the right end for a two-point conversion to make the score 15–0.

Falk knew that the Buckeyes were starting to feel desperate when Woody would not allow the Michigan ball boys to stand at the line of scrimmage. Each team is allowed to have two ball boys on the opposing side of the field. They are responsible for quickly getting a fresh ball into play for the offense. "Woody wouldn't allow them inside the 30-yard line," Falk said. "He didn't want any Michigan people walking in front of his bench. Somehow Woody got it into his head that the boys were stealing signs and relaying them to our coaches. Every time we had a ball exchange, we couldn't get it in fast enough because the boys weren't on the line of scrimmage."

Falk tried to diplomatically settle the problem by talking to Ohio State equipment manager John Bozick. "If somebody has to stand next to our ball boy, that's fine," Falk told Bozick. "But we've got to get a fresh ball into the game. I know it's tough to talk to Coach Hayes now, but something needs to be done."

Bozick looked at Falk and laughed. "We're in the middle of a game," Bozick said. "We're at home...we're playing Michigan...we're losing...*and you want me to go talk to Coach Hayes?*"

Falk could certainly identify with his friend's prickly predicament. "All I'm saying is we've got to be able to get our balls into the game, or we're not gonna let your boys on our sideline either," Falk said. Somehow the sticky situation seemed to settle itself. Wet or dry balls, on that day it didn't seem to matter for Michigan.

The kicking team had practiced the two-point conversion play the previous week. A Michigan victory meant both teams would finish 7–1 in the Big Ten. Michigan would get the Rose Bowl nod for winning the head-to-head competition, and Bo was taking no chances. Michigan scored again in the fourth quarter to make the final score 22–0. Earlier in the week *Detroit Free Press* sportswriter Joe Falls wrote a column predicting Michigan would beat Ohio State 21–0. "See what I've always told you, Jon?" Bo said to Falk after the game. "Those sportswriters don't know anything. Ol' Bo had a little surprise for them today with that two-point conversion."

Bo devoted a portion of practice to game-planning for Ohio State each day of the season. Of course, when rivalry week with Ohio State rolled around, all the football facilities and offices transformed into war-time battle stations. Bo was as meticulously thorough at providing for his team as he was in his relentless drilling of the offensive line.

For 15 minutes before every practice—regardless of the upcoming opponent—Michigan would simulate the Ohio State punting game against the Wolverine punt return unit using the JUGS machine that Jon purchased. It would shoot out 40- to 50-yard spirals, and Jimmy Smith would pick his way through tacklers behind the wall of blockers in front.

During the Ohio State game, Smith and his bruising buddies in front of him made the JUGS machine purchase well worth every penny. OSU's Tom Skladany punted the ball eight times for a 52.2-yard average. Smith negated the brilliant performance by gobbling up 91 yards in punt returns to keep Michigan in good field position. "That's what it takes to be a great football coach," Falk said. "The great ones always look ahead. Bo knew every player on the Ohio State roster like he knew the telephone number of his mother. That was every year. Even when he got out of coaching, no one came close to outworking Bo in any way. He never knew any other way."

Chapter 20
Tom Brady and Barry Larkin

Often Jon Falk's support to the players on the team dealt with attitude adjustment and not just football particulars.

It doesn't seem that long ago that Big Jon spent a lot of time in the locker room trying to convince a future Hall of Famer that his time at Michigan as the starting quarterback was coming soon. Tom Brady was feeling anxious about having to sit on the bench. In the meantime, Falk worked hard at convincing him that once he secured the job it would be his until it was time to move up to the pros. Until then, he had to work hard every day to show the coaches and players he is a natural leader.

Falk was a master with the football team and also appreciated all of the athletes at Michigan.

Steve Everitt was an All-American center at Michigan before spending seven years in the NFL after being a first round draft pick in 1993 by the Cleveland Browns. Everitt was born and raised in Miami, Florida, and was a Michigan fan throughout his youth. He couldn't wait for his first opportu-

Tom Brady gives a lot of credit to Big Jon for helping him mature as a man.

nity to meet Bo when he got to Ann Arbor and had the chance to fulfill his dream.

Soon thereafter, Everitt was introduced to another Michigan legend who wound up being a lifelong friend. "I walked into the weight room and spotted this guy who looked big enough to be a player," Everitt said. "He was running on the treadmill and was sweating profusely. We wound up becoming friends for life."

It didn't take long for Falk to realize how much impact Everitt made for the Michigan team, and it didn't take long for Everitt to appreciate what a talented jack-of-all-trades Falk was to the whole team. Everitt became forever grateful to Falk when Falk devised a protective device that prevented the All-American center from missing any starts with a broken jaw. "I never saw anyone who knows more about the university and all of its traditions," Everitt said. "And I never met anyone who could recite University of Michigan traditions as quickly and perfectly as Jon. Big Jon has that dramatic tone in his voice when he starts talking about Michigan. He taught all of us as freshmen about the Little Brown Jug tradition with the University of Minnesota. He taught us about the Paul Bunyan Trophy with Michigan State. He taught us how to sing 'The Victors' and the magic of running through that tunnel in The Big House and all of the All-Americans that ran through it since it was built.

"Most of all he taught all of us the meaning of 'the team, the team, the team' that Bo stressed every day. Jon tells stories so easily that it seems like he's reading them off a page. He actually paints pictures with his words. I hope there are at least a few people around to carry the tradition that Big Jon began. He should never be forgotten. He's a very special man in a program that has generated so many immortal traditions."

Even a Hall of Fame athlete needs a few words of meaningful guidance once in a while—especially one so gifted in athletics that he could have made a living playing baseball or football following graduation. And he had to make a choice. That's how talented Barry Larkin was during his stay at the University of Michigan.

Recruited by coaches from nearly every powerful athletic program in the country for both sports, Larkin was a flat out blue-chip special. He was so special that it was difficult for Falk to determine at which sport Larkin would be most successful. In football Larkin was a spine-rattling safety whom Bo recruited hard to play in those trademark maize and blue uniforms with those unmistakable maize stripes shining boldly from the tops of the helmets. In baseball Larkin was a natural fixture at shortstop, where he gobbled up grounders anywhere between second and third base.

During the '80s before football became a year-round commitment for all the players, Falk enjoyed serving the baseball team in the same position as his football involvement. He views each athlete who has earned the privilege of wearing the Michigan uniform as special in the sport of his or her choice.

He relished any opportunity to share a life lesson in his unofficial role as the keeper of Michigan tradition. "At Michigan we take great pride in the entire athletic program," Falk said. "We recognize how athletic excellence can help performance in the real world after graduation. It helped Barry to get a little experience in sports and life."

At the Baseball Hall of Fame induction ceremonies in 2012 in Cooperstown, New York, Larkin publicly expressed his gratitude to Bo and Big Jon in his acceptance speech. It's quite an honor to the memory of Bo, and Falk will embrace that moment for as long as he lives. "I used to joke with Bo that his best football decision was to let me play baseball," Larkin said. "And Big Jon…there'll never be enough words to thank you and all you did for me and the entire athletic program."

One of those valuable life lessons learned at the University of Michigan sprung out of a dusty and bumpy Mississippi State University baseball diamond where the University of Michigan baseball team, including Larkin, a once-in-a-lifetime shortstop phenom out of Cincinnati, Ohio, was playing in a tournament. He successfully pursued the game tirelessly and capped his Cincinnati Reds career with election into the Baseball Hall of Fame and later the state of Michigan Sports Hall of Fame.

The perpetrator of what could have degenerated into an ugly situation was a foulmouthed jerk sitting in the stands. Larkin was the lone African American on the field, and the ignorant blabbermouth situated down the third-base line was relentless with his racist nonsensical jabber. "I was ready to head down the line and settle everything right there," Larkin recalled. "I was reaching that point of no return. Then Big Jon grabbed my arm and shook some sense into me. He told me I could knock the babbling bigot into next Tuesday, but what was that gonna prove? And who was gonna pay for that? Why not just take it out on the other team on the field? Show them how little common sense and human decency some of those fans had. Beat 'em on the field and then walk away proudly."

And that's exactly what Larkin did. By the end of the tournament,

Former All-American center Steve Everitt, who learned how to sing "The Victors" from Jon Falk, holds a Bo Schembechler bobblehead in the Michigan room at his home in the Florida Keys.

Larkin and the Wolverines thoroughly defeated the overmatched opponent, and Larkin wound up as the MVP of the tournament. And there were so many more awards that Larkin collected as one of Michigan's all-time greatest baseball players that it's tough to find trophy space in his home. Thanks to Falk's quick thinking, the incident was squelched as quickly as one of Larkin's rocket throws from the hole at shortstop to first base.

Falk first met Larkin when he was a freshman on the baseball field. Bo wanted to sign him to a football scholarship, but as hard as Bo tried, Barry wanted to play just baseball. He was strong. He was fast. He was one of those natural-born athletes who could have excelled in the sport of his choice. "Barry was quick," Falk confirmed. "And he could stick. Man, it was fun to watch him play any sport."

Larkin's love for baseball, however, led him into a career that he dreamed about since he was a little boy. "I'll never forget Big Jon for all the favors he did for me during my time at Michigan," Larkin said. "It didn't matter what sport a student-athlete played as long as that athlete represented Michigan properly. I really loved when Big Jon came to a game in Cincinnati to see me during the season playing with the Reds. He always came with a few new jokes stuffed inside his pockets. Always made you laugh. He's the kind of guy you keep in your heart forever. He helped out a lot of young players in a variety of sports. A lot of guys felt more comfortable talkin' to Jon rather than the coaches. He really took a liking to every player that wore the maize and blue. I honestly don't think there's anyone who has a greater love for Michigan than Jon Falk."

Falk was far more than a mere equipment manager, according to Larkin. "Big Jon did so much for all the players, Larkin said. "He was a mentor who connected the dots between the players and the coaches. I always felt comfortable talking to Big Jon more than I did to the coaches."

Larkin credits the university for helping him to mature into a man. "I was blessed with some great mentors," Larkin said in his acceptance speech at the large assembly of fans at the Baseball Hall of Fame in Cooperstown. "Bo had a big influence on me. So did Jon Falk."

Chapter **21**

How 'Bout Them Boots?

Early in the 1988 season, Jon Falk popped into Bo's office one morning merely to say hello. Without any prompting his eyes were drawn to Bo's feet—or more specifically—what was on them. "Wow, Bo," Falk said with surprise. "You've got yourself a new pair of boots."

Not just any pair of boots. They were black and made of genuine leather. They looked like those worn by John Wayne in one of his signature western movies. They had pointed toes, and "Bo" was hand-carved on both sides of each boot. "Somebody must have given those to you because you wouldn't spend what those things cost," Falk teased. "I could buy a dozen pairs of sneakers for what those babies must cost."

Bo lifted his pants to give Falk the full effect. "Wish you had these, don't you?" Bo said. "Only the cowboys at heart can wear these things."

The boots were sent by Dallas Cowboys executive Gil Brandt. Bo knew all the important people in the NFL.

Later that afternoon, the assistant coaches arrived early in the locker room to prepare for the daily meeting with players from respective units.

Bo Schembechler congratulates his good friend, Jon Falk, during Big Jon's wedding.

Falk was busy tending to all his duties in the locker room when he got called to Bo's office. "Falk, get in here," Bo yelled. "I need your help with something."

When Bo spotted Falk nearing his office, again he yelled to "get in here right now—and close that door."

Falk looked back over his shoulder and then squarely at Bo. "Now wait a minute, Bo," he said tentatively. "You and I are in this locker room alone, and I have to shut the door? What's goin' on here?"

Falk recognized the squint Bo got in his eyes whenever he was serious. "What I'm asking you to do is something I want you never to tell anyone," Bo said. "You never tell anyone what you're about to do for me."

Falk didn't squint. In fact, his eyes almost popped from their sockets. "Bo, you're getting me a little nervous," he said. "Now just what do you have in mind?"

Though no one else was in the room, Bo lowered his voice and said, "Get these damn boots off my feet. I can't get them to budge."

Finally, Falk could smile. In fact, he broke into a boisterous belly laugh.

Even with Falk's strength he had to struggle with the boots. Falk turned his back to Bo, put both legs over Bo's knees, and bent forward as if he were riding a horse. It was, to say the least, an outrageously compromising position. "Now Bo, if anyone walks in here while we're in this position, we're gonna have a little explaining to do," Falk said.

Bo broke into a roar at the same time one of the boots popped from his foot. With the proper technique now discovered, Falk hurriedly removed the second one. "Bo was beautiful," Falk said. "He was tough and could be ornery, but he had the innocence of a boy in his heart. He could see the humor in life, and I think that's what helped him to be able to laugh at himself."

Chapter **22**
Did You Rob That Bank?

Waiting for that single opportunity to play in a game for the University of Michigan demands dedication, perseverance, and patience. Once in a while it even requires a trip to the local police department to prove your innocence in a bank robbery charge.

At least that's the way it happened for Pat Moons, who made the most of his opportunity to kick against Ohio State in the victory that sent the Wolverines to the 1986 Fiesta Bowl. Moons was a place-kicker who had never seen the field before his senior year in 1985. A good student and reliable member of the team, he showed up slightly late for practice before the fourth game.

Jon Falk had to return to the locker room to retrieve a piece of equipment. When he walked through the door, he thought he had entered *The Twilight Zone*. There were two members of the local SWAT team, three Ann Arbor police officers, and three university police officers. All had weapons drawn and aimed at one young man in the middle.

Falk knew all the officers and couldn't understand why they had weapons drawn inside of his locker room. And why were they pointed at one of the members of the team? "What's going on here, guys?" Falk asked.

"We've got a bank robber here, Jon," one of them barked. "Stand back. We don't want anyone hurt."

Straining to see the surrounded suspect, Falk broke into a laugh when he recognized the face. "That's no bank robber," he said confidently. "That's Pat Moons. He's a kicker on the team."

The officers were not swayed. "We're sorry, Jon," one said. "He's been positively identified for robbing a bank here in Ann Arbor, and we're gonna have to arrest him and take him in."

Falk was as equally determined as the officers. "This isn't right," he said. This is just not right. This is not a bank robber. This is Pat Moons. He's a kicker on the Michigan football team."

Big Jon ran out to the practice field faster than anyone playing in the backfield could. It was time to bring Bo into the situation. "Bo, the police are arresting Pat Moons for robbing a bank," Falk said.

Bo looked at Falk as if he had told him that he had just swallowed a football. "What the hell are you talkin' about?" Bo asked. "Are you goin' crazy on me now here during practice?"

Falk managed to convince Bo to return to the locker room. On the way he told Bo to be careful because all the weapons were drawn. "What the hell is goin' on here?" Bo demanded upon entering the room.

"Bo, we have a positive ID that this man here robbed a bank in Ann Arbor," one of the officers said.

Bo walked up to Moons and stared straight into his eyes. "Moons," he said. "Did you just rob a damn bank?"

"No sir," he said. "I was at the bank. That's why I was late. But I sure didn't rob it."

Bo turned to all the police officers and raised his arms as if he had just cracked a case easier than a peanut shell. "There you have it men," he said confidently. "Pat Moons said he did not rob the bank. You have the wrong man. Now all of us have to get back to practice."

Smiling slightly, one of the officers told Bo they still had to take Moons to the station in order to clear the matter. Bo didn't like it, but he told Moons to go with the officers peacefully, and everything would be worked out. "The law will take care of itself," Bo said. "You'll be alright. I'll talk to you later, Moons."

Moons, in fact, had been at the bank that was robbed. A witness had seen Moons running to his car, but that's because he was late for practice. However, the identification of him as being the robber was incorrect.

As the season progressed—with no bank robbery charge hanging over his head—Moons continued to practice patiently and got the surprise of his career on the Saturday Michigan hosted Ohio State at The Big House.

Mike Gillette, the gifted place-kicker who handled all kicking duties, broke a team rule on the Friday before the game with Ohio State. "That was one thing with Bo that never changed," Falk said. "If a player broke a team rule, he had to suffer the consequences. It didn't matter who the player was—first stringer or walk-on who had splinters from sitting on the bench. Bo never bent the rules for anyone."

Gillette was benched for the biggest game of the season. After four years of waiting, Moons was in the game. "I can't even imagine what was going through his mind the first time he took the field," Falk said. "He had never stepped on the grass during a game and now he was out there against Ohio State. Whatever was going through his mind sure turned out to be pretty good."

Moons kicked two field goals and converted on all three extra-point attempts as Michigan dumped the Buckeyes 27–17.

The only major glitch in that season came at Iowa in the sixth game on the schedule. Stories by then had circulated from Iowa that coach Hayden Fry had the visitors' locker room painted totally in pink. Apparently it was a psychological ploy to subconsciously make the visitors more docile and less enthusiastic about playing a hard-nosed game.

When confronted by an attack—physical or psychological—Bo always had a counter. "Now you know the locker room we're going to be using is pink," Bo said to Falk early in the week. "When you get down there, I want you to go out and buy all the butcher's paper you need to cover every inch of that room, I mean every inch. I don't want to see one speck of pink."

Falk took a deep breath. "My God, Bo," Falk said. "That's an awful lot of footage to cover in just one day."

Bo eyed him and then repeated his command. "I want every inch covered with white paper," he said. "Remember—no pink! I know I have the right man for the job."

Falk purchased eight rolls of white butcher's paper as soon as he arrived in Iowa Friday morning. He and three student assistants finished the job before the team arrived.

Bo walked the entire room inspecting each inch like a grizzled drill sergeant. "Good job, Jon," he said.

And that was it.

Iowa entered the game rated No. 1 in the country. Michigan was No. 2. At the time, it was only the 19th time in NCAA history for such a meeting to occur. The Wolverines rolled into Iowa City with a defense that had allowed only one touchdown in five games. The D extended that mark to one in six games before they left. However, the Hawkeyes kicked four field goals and hung on for a 12–10 victory. The only other smudge on the Michigan record was a 3–3 tie at Illinois.

On the trip back to Ann Arbor, Bo dismissed the mystique of the pink. "That loss had nothing to do with anything in the locker room," Bo said. "They simply outplayed us."

With the victory over Ohio State, Michigan finished the regular season with a 9-1-1 mark and a berth in the Fiesta Bowl against highly regarded Nebraska. A stellar defense and a 24-point third quarter explosion again powered the Wolverines to a 27–23 victory. Moons kicked two more field goals and added three extra points.

Chapter **23**

Enemy Found
and Captured

hree days before going to Columbus, Bo and Falk had to defuse an interesting case of subterfuge in Ann Arbor. At Tuesday's practice, which marked the first day of hitting, Falk noticed a red light beaming from the second story of a house on State Street across from the practice field. As the offense moved the ball down the field, the beam of light curiously followed. "Hey Coach," Falk said, "I think there's a camera up in that window."

Bo dispatched Falk to investigate. Falk ran across the street and knocked loudly on the door. When no one answered, he shouted, "Sir, if you have a camera and are taking pictures, we are not allowing that today."

A voice shouted back at Falk: "Go away…this is private property."

Falk reported back to Bo, and the two raced across the street. Bo was slightly less diplomatic. "Open this damn door!" Bo shouted. "You're not taking pictures of our practice during Ohio State week. I want that camera."

A voice again responded, "Go away. I called the police. I'm not opening the door 'til the police get here."

That wasn't a good enough answer for Bo. "I want this damn door open and I want it opened now!"

At that moment, an Ann Arbor police officer was walking up the steps. "What's going on here, Bo?" the officer asked.

Bo explained the situation and told the officer he wanted that camera confiscated "immediately." The door slowly opened. Falk sensed the man inside figured the officer would protect him from Bo. "Give me those films and camera," the officer demanded.

The man argued that the material was private property. "Oh, we'll give them back," the officer said. "We're just going to hold on to them…until Sunday."

Bo never allowed interviews or pictures of his players the week before the Ohio State showdown. He believed those pictures would land in the hands of coach Woody Hayes. Both coaches worked hard to keep battle plans secret for the Saturday showdown. So when Bo got wind that the incident had been initiated by the United Press International (UPI), he was still angry by Monday's weekly meeting with the press. "Anybody here that represents UPI better get out," he began even before discussing Saturday's victory. "I am not talking to you. No press person is ever gonna take pictures of us practicing. Especially not before the Ohio State game."

Chapter **24**

A Football Dream

Bo had a dream to build a new football building that would be the best in the college football. When he was athletic director, he began to work on his plans for the new building. Bo was determined to get the facility completed as much as he loved beating Ohio State...well, maybe not that much.

He led the campaign, a major undertaking, to have one of the nation's most beautiful football buildings in the country. Jon Falk got an up-close look at Bo's determination. "He called upon everyone he knew to support the drive for a new facility," Falk said. "After all, who was going to say no to Bo?"

At the end of the 1988 season, all the football operations were moved to the football stadium, and Michigan used the visitors' and home locker rooms for practice. Everyone moved to the home-side for gamedays. While the team was using the stadium, demolition of the old building began. It was later renamed Schembechler Hall and remains one of the jewels in college football.

Anthony Thomas, the bruising running back who rushed for 4,472 yards at Michigan, inadvertently led to the creation of a new medical room. (Courtesy University of Michigan Athletic Department)

The new building would have an area that another player, Anthony Thomas, gave genesis to—albeit in a completely different way. "When the Board of Regents approved a new locker room in 2002," Falk said, "one of the first additions was a new medical room where it would have a clean room for doctors to visit and be able to perform minor surgical repairs."

The A-Train, one of the greatest runners in Michigan history, inadvertently led to that new medical room. "In the Illinois game in 1999, we were up 27–7 before Anthony got hurt," Falk said. "We were in our old locker room at the stadium and didn't have a clean room for doctors. We had to send Anthony to the hospital to have a laceration sewn together for him. By the time Anthony got back for the game, we lost to Illinois 35–29…Because of the 1999 game, we nicknamed the room the Anthony Thomas Room."

Chapter **25**
A Fitting Farewell

Jon Falk's farewell tour with the 2013 Michigan football team certainly lacked the dramatics of the full season send-off to Hall of Fame-bound New York Yankees shortstop Derek Jeter that played coast to coast in 2014.

And rightly so.

But for the 40 years that Michigan teams were served by Falk and for all die-hard Wolverine fans scattered throughout the country, memories of the locker room legend will stay forever young. For his peculiarities, his passion for Michigan football, and his appreciation for what that program means for Michigan faithful across the globe, Falk has left a mark on the proud football program that is likely to live forever.

And just for the record, Jeter—who grew up in Kalamazoo, Michigan—and Falk do share a friendship that dates back to when Jeter was toying with becoming a Wolverine on a baseball scholarship before the Yankees dropped a whole lot of pennies from heaven to get his signature on one of the most rewarding signings in the history of the game. Jeter was close to signing a tender with the Wolverines but finally decided to accept "an offer he couldn't refuse" from the Yankees.

Falk secured a sideline pass for Jeter whenever his schedule allowed him to come to a game at The Big House. "He's one of the most talented and personable young men anyone could have the good fortune of meeting," Falk said. "He was mature far beyond his years. He would have made a wonderful Wolverine, but there's no doubt he made the right choice."

During one Yankees visit to Comerica Park, third baseman Alex Rodriguez visited the Michigan athletic facilities. Before leaving the Michigan complex, Rodriguez was given a Michigan T-shirt by Falk. "Here, Alex," Falk said. "Jeter will cry if he sees you got one and he didn't."

On a far lesser scale, of course, Falk enjoyed an almost dream-like experience as he went through his final season as the proudest football equipment manager anywhere in the country. "I was overwhelmed by some of the good wishes from so many fans and friends," Falk said. "I'll forever be moved by their courtesy and support for Michigan football. It all goes back to Bo. To the assistant coaches. The staff. The players. The fans. Most of all I thank the great University of Michigan, which made it all possible. Bo taught all of us the same thing: 'no player, no coach, no staff member, no administrator is bigger than the team…the team…the team.' That's something he let no one forget."

Falk was the 1974 founding member of the College Football Equipment Managers Association of America, and news of his retirement spread quickly across the nation. Falk was one of seven founding fathers and served as executive director in 1986 through 2010. He was named the Athletic Equipment Managers Association (AEMA) Equipment Manager of the Year in 2001 and awarded the Lifetime Achievement Award in 2005.

Falk had become a Michigan icon. Somehow, some way, it was expected that he should never be able to leave. Letters, phone calls, and emails were overwhelming during that first week after the announcement. From those managers within the Big Ten, tokens of their appreciation were sent to Big Jon as a symbol to his dedication and loyalty to the profession.

Michigan State basketball coach Tom Izzo, a good friend of Jon Falk, made sure to meet up with Big Jon during Falk's final trip to East Lansing as Michigan equipment manager.

Some sent their official school's hat. Some sent T-shirts. Some sent jerseys with the appropriate No. 40 sewn to the back. Longtime friend and Michigan State University equipment manager Bob Knickerbocker invited Falk to a luncheon in a meeting room on the Spartans' side of the field when the two teams played in East Lansing. "Just the two of us," Falk said, "we can have some toast and coffee and laugh about all the good times we were lucky to have had."

Little did Falk know that a slightly more elaborate venue already had been prepared. Knickerbocker and his assistants were there. So was Michigan State athletic director Mark Hollis and his assistant Greg Ianni. Perhaps the biggest surprise to Falk was Tom Izzo waiting at the door to congratulate his longtime friend. "He's an awful big man to take time out from his busy schedule for doing this for me," Falk said. "We've been friends for a long time, but I never expected this."

Izzo then crowned Falk with perhaps the highest compliment he could bestow. "Forty years as football equipment manager for the University of Michigan," Izzo said with a tone of reverence in his voice, "Jon has earned every honor he's received. He's a Michigan icon, a true professional, an ambassador for the university. Even more importantly, I'm proud he is a friend of mine. He deserves every honor he's ever gotten."

Michigan State gave a miniature Paul Bunyan Trophy that reads: "A great Wolverine and competitor for 40 years. Thank you for your true friendship to the Spartan family." "No one will ever know how much good Jon has done for every person in that program," Izzo said. "That's because he learned from the best. He was taught by Bo Schembechler. He's one of Bo's boys."

The final game of the 2013 regular season was one of the most moving experiences Falk has ever experienced. During one of the practices before the annual Ohio State-Michigan bash, coach Brady Hoke called the team for a brief meeting on the field. He told the team that 40 years at any place is a tremendous achievement. He told them 40 years at Michigan is almost impossible. Then he told them what he was going to do. "We're going to make Jon an honorary captain for that game," Hoke shouted to the team.

When the day came, the team exploded from the Tunnel in a heart-felt convergence of unity. Those players closest to him on the field probably heard Falk's heart pounding. They also could see the tears trickling down his cheeks in a steady drip. "I thanked Brady and the team," Falk said. "I remember charging out of the Tunnel and then reminding myself not to stumble. I remember walking out to the middle of the field for the coin flip moments before the game. Then I remember asking myself what the heck was I doing here? As the visiting team, Ohio State had the privilege of making the call. They called tails. Same call I would have made."

Upon his retirement Big Jon was presented with a miniature Paul Bunyan Trophy from Michigan State equipment manager Bob Knickerbocker.

A few days later, former Michigan quarterback Tom Brady called Falk to remind him what he had once told the four-time Super Bowl winner. "When you're captain of the Michigan football team, it's one of those things you never forget," Brady told him. "It's something you live with the rest of your life."

Upon the first timeout of that game, the gigantic electronic scoreboards featured former Michigan head coaches Gary Moeller, Lloyd Carr, and Hoke reminiscing about Big Jon Falk. "One of the toughest parts of that day was getting out of the Tunnel and across the field without falling flat on my face," Falk said. "When you come out of that tunnel knowing it's your last time, you get a little worried. That's how every senior feels on that day. All the previous times, you don't really think about it because you figure there will always be next year. But when you know it's your last time down that tunnel, it's a very emotional feeling knowing that when you run out of there it'll be the last time you will be touching that 'M Go Blue' Banner in front of more than 100,000 people, kind of makes you want to cry. And, as a matter of fact, I did cry."

Despite the 42–41 heartbreaking loss to Ohio State, Falk became the focus of the locker room. Players surrounded him to say good-bye or get a picture of him with themselves.

Now with no more games in The Big House to ever prepare for, Falk—as usual—mentally started to get ready for the final game of his long and distinguished career. That was against Kansas State, which defeated Michigan 31–14 on December 28 in the Buffalo Wild Wings Bowl in Tempe, Arizona. "I knew it was my last game, but I didn't know how I was supposed to feel," Falk said. "In some ways I felt relieved. In other ways I felt confused and alone. When your entire adult life is founded on one of the most prestigious and trusted universities in the nation with one of the nation's most highly regarded football teams, it's impossible to simply flip a switch and say good-bye. I know for sure I've got bushels full of memories that will keep my heart warm forever. That's what 40 years do. And I'm so grateful."

Returning from the bowl game against Kansas State, Falk had to complete a lot of office work before turning over his keys to new equipment manager Brad Berlin. It's a whole lot easier to close the books on one season than the previous 39. Falk had keys to every office in Schembechler Hall—and even The Big House itself. They were precious to Falk. They validated the trust that the university had in him. He carried those keys on a ring that must have weighed a couple of pounds. He carried those keys wherever he went and never let them leave his sight.

On February 27, 2014, Falk had completed the cleaning of his office and tossed the key ring to Berlin. "They come and they go, Hobbs," Falk smiled at Berlin. "They come and they go."

Chapter **26**

Forty Years of Memories

Memories are the street signs for the paths we have chosen to travel through life. Some are happy. Some are sad. They are what we make of them. And winners almost always make the most. Drifting back slowly on his 40-year career at the University of Michigan, Jon Falk shakes his head and marvels at where all of those years have gone. The memories remain in our hearts. They become part of the spirit that we carry. They're priceless.

Ann Arbor, where Falk has lived since 1974, is an irresistibly charming American college town, a Norman Rockwell natural, a true memory-making machine. On a crisp autumn sunny football Saturday, the changing leaves of red, green, orange, brown, and yellow cling to the branches of their trees before dropping gently from the sky. As the football season moves swiftly from start to finish, the fallen leaves lie quietly until crunched under the foot traffic of loyalists going to the games. The melodies played by the Michigan Marching Band fill the air as does the mixed aroma of hot dogs, burgers, and a variety of tailgate specialties too numerous to mention all.

Having worked all but one Michigan football game since his arrival to the program in 1974, Falk's football Saturday perspective is shared only by a fortunate few—in the locker room and on the field. That's quite a restricted perspective which Falk never took for granted.

Through his 40-year run as the Michigan equipment manager, Jon missed only one game. The single game that Jon missed occurred on October 29, 2005. The previous Saturday on October 22, Falk suffered a broken leg at Iowa on a freak sideline collision with a Hawkeyes player. Falk was taken to the hospital and was back at the stadium before the game was finished. His leg was wrapped tightly, and there were tears in his eyes when coach Lloyd Carr boarded the team plane and went directly to see him. "A lot of pain?" Carr asked.

"No," Falk answered quickly. "I'm cryin' because I'm gonna miss my first Michigan game next Saturday."

The Iowa game had been on national TV, so many of Falk's friends had witnessed the accidental hit. Telegrams and phone calls began to flood into the hospital even before Falk had arrived. Rick Leach was the first one to get through. Bo and Cathy came to visit him that evening. As the week progressed, messages began to pile up. One even came from President George W. Bush.

Here are more stories that will forever fill Falk's bank of memories.

1974

No one ever forgets their first football game at Michigan Stadium. For a player, coach, or fan, it's one of the state's most exciting and lasting memories. It's like celebrating your 21st birthday or your 65th retirement party. Whether you're calling plays from the sidelines or selling peanuts on the street, that first game at The Big House is forever memorable and remains fresh in the mind as if it had been played last week.

It was Jon Falk's first Big Ten game, the first time in attendance in a stadium that seated more than 76,000.

And Falk experienced something none of those 76,802 fans could ever

THE WHITE HOUSE

WASHINGTON

November 15, 2005

Mr. Jon Falk
1373 Armstrong Drive
Chelsea, Michigan 48118

Dear Jon:

Laura and I wanted to send you a letter of encouragement. You are in
our thoughts and prayers.

We hope the support of your family and friends is of great comfort to
you during this difficult time. Your strength and determination
demonstrate the American spirit. May God bless you and your family.

Sincerely,

George W. Bush

*President George W. Bush sent Jon Falk a letter of encouragement upon learning that Big
Jon broke his leg against Iowa.*

imagine doing. It was his first trip down the Tunnel—that mysterious cloak
of darkness that connects the locker room to the field, which looks bigger
than the sky and all of the clouds above.

The timing of that trip through the Tunnel couldn't have been more
dramatically placed. It came directly after Bo had finished a blood-rushing
pregame talk that made every person on the team feel that the darkness was
actually their friend. To run through that tunnel…to hear the band playing
down on the field…to hear the band singing "The Victors"…to hear the

deafening chants of "Go Blue, Go" as it echoed in the Tunnel as the players came out of the locker room and down to the field. That's a big menu to fill!

This was all serious mind-boggling stuff for someone working a game in The Big House for the first time.

As the team ran through the Tunnel, all the players were jumping up to touch that "Go Blue" banner. People cheered wildly as the seconds ticked down to the start of the game. The fans were deliriously hungry for the return of Michigan football. "What a great experience it was for me," Falk marveled now 40 years later. "To be honest I was a little intimidated and scared cuz that was an amazing feeling to come out of the darkness of the Tunnel and see the sunlight. At one point while running, I thought I was going to be magically lifted toward the sky and simply fly across the field. I had to keep reminding myself not to trip and fall down in front of all these people. There was so much maize and blue throughout the entire stadium. Even high up in the press box, the colors proudly showed themselves."

Before 76,802 people in the stadium, Michigan sent a message to Iowa with the 24–7 win. It was easy to tell from that first game that Michigan was going to be a factor again in the Big Ten. "What a great experience...something I'll never forget as long as I live. But then just the opposite happens at the end of the season when we go down to Columbus, Ohio. They always said when I grew up in Oxford, Ohio, that I must know three things about Michigan: Bo was the football coach, everybody in Ohio hates Michigan, and Michigan and Ohio State play every year for the Big Ten championship. I learned real fast when we went down to Columbus, Ohio, that not many people in that stadium of 88,243 people liked Michigan. They were loudly against Michigan the whole game. They love their Buckeyes the same way Michigan fans love their Wolverines."

1975

Sometimes the promise of a bright future is worth the pain of getting there. A preseason injury to quarterback Mark Elzinga threatened to turn hope

Big Jon prepares for his first day on the job at Michigan during his rookie season in 1974.

into despair. But Bo had the guts to put Rick Leach into the starting lineup, and the freshman quarterback showed poise and daring to save the young season before it sped out of control.

Leach grabbed control of the team in the rugged season opener at Wisconsin, a perilous place to play even for the most experienced quarterback. The 79,000 rabid fans at Wisconsin have a way of intimidating even a veteran team with poise and experience. "We all were concerned," Jon Falk said. "As we packed for the trip, we kept thinking about Leach and how he would handle that rowdy crowd. *How is he going to silence all those bleacher-shaking band of headhunters?* Well, he played pretty good."

The entire staff discovered quickly that Leach was a competitor who refused to be intimidated. Michigan won 23–6. And as the season progressed, Leach demonstrated he would not be lifted from the quarterback position. He was on the fast track to becoming one of the school's all-time finest. In the final regular season game at Ohio State, Michigan went ahead 14–7 in the fourth quarter, and Leach had outplayed Buckeyes great Cornelius Green. "We got beat 21–14, but we learned that we were starting to have a real great quarterback for the next three years." Falk said.

1976

At the beginning of the 1976 August camp, Bo casually walked up to Jon Falk and nonchalantly asked him a rhetorical question. "You do understand that we play Ohio State this year in Columbus for the Big Ten championship, don't you, Jon Falk?"

Falk immediately nodded his head several times and said: "Affirmative, sir."

"Well, I want you to know they have a great punter there named Tom Skladany," Bo said. "I also want you to know that we have to learn how to return the punts from this man so that when we go down to Columbus we win the Big Ten championship. But Lord knows we don't have anybody that can kick the ball 45 or 50 yards in the air. Now what are we going to do about that, Falk?"

Falk kept himself abreast of all the latest football equipment and told Bo about the JUGS machine that can be geared to regularly replicate a punt of at least 50 yards.

The conversation didn't last long. "Go get us one of those machines," Bo said. "I want it here by tomorrow."

Falk realized then that here's a man who was studying Ohio State all summer after the '75 season and knew their strengths in August of 1976. The Wolverines began to practice every day with that punting machine. Jimmy Smith was returning those punts because Bo knew that if they could return those punts they could equalize the game down in Columbus.

The key to the Michigan 22–0 victory was that Jimmy Smith had 91 yards in punt returns to negate a brilliant 52.2 yard average punt by Skladany. That alone took Ohio State's best punter out of the game. The 22–0 shutout was Bo's first victory in Columbus.

1977

The Wolverines were ranked No. 1 in the country when they went to Minnesota in 1977 for the annual battle for the Little Brown Jug. "We had probably one of our best teams," Jon Falk said. "By the time we left, we were soaked and knocked from the top."

On Friday afternoon the sun was out. It was a nice, beautiful day, about 80 degrees. Bo told Falk that Minnesota was going to water the field, and it would be ready for the next day's game. Minnesota promised to suck out any standing water. "They don't have a sucking machine here," Falk told Bo. "That water is going stay in the Earth for as long as it decides to."

Bo was convinced the water situation was going to be settled before the start of the game.

"Look Falk," Bo growled. "The man told me that the water would be gone. It will be gone."

The next morning Falk went to the football stadium at 6:30 AM. When he approached the field, the sprinklers were still running on the field. The water had overflowed onto the track at Minnesota's stadium. Falk called athletic director Paul Giel at home and told him that the water had destroyed the field. Finally they got the sprinklers shut off. At 11:00 AM Schembechler showed up. He walked onto the field, and his dress shoes sank about an inch into the mud. Bo looked up at Falk and said, "We're in trouble today, Jon…deep, deep trouble."

With a great and speedy running back named Harlan Huckleby and the quick Rick Leach at quarterback Michigan's game plan was running to the outside. That's not an easy task with the field under water. Minnesota had big burly guys inside to stop the game. With that muddy and wet field, Michigan slipped and sloshed around all day. With one-and-a-half minutes left in the game, Michigan was down 16–0. Minnesota fans started screaming, "We want the jug, we want the jug." Their voices echoed in Falk's head the whole night after that game. When those players from Minnesota came over and grabbed that jug, he knew then how valuable that little brown jug is to Michigan and Minnesota.

1978

There's as much of a mystique surrounding Notre Dame as there is about Michigan football. There was an added dash of that mystique in the boiling pot for the first game between the giants when Michigan traveled to Notre Dame Stadium in South Bend for the first time since 1943.

The renewal of the rivalry between college football's two winningest programs was extra special that year because of the two competing quarterbacks, who were among the best in the country. The Fighting Irish featured future Hall of Famer Joe Montana. The Wolverines countered with Rick Leach, who was in his senior year, against Joe Montana. Michigan won the game 28–14 on the strength of Leach's arm and his ability to run the ball. It was one of the best games of the entire football season.

1979

Who would have thought that Michigan's biggest game of the season and arguably one of the biggest games in Michigan history would come against

Anthony Carter, who had 3,076 receiving yards during his Michigan career, produced one of the most memorable plays in Michigan history to help defeat Indiana in 1979. (Courtesy University of Michigan Athletic Department)

Indiana? Over the 100 seasons that Michigan has played football, no game offered more excitement than this Hoosiers-Wolverines showdown in a game that was supposed to be in Michigan's back pocket.

Fifty-five seconds were left on the clock when the impossible dream was being put together in front of another sold-out crowd in The Big House. Quarterback John Wangler and freshman wide receiver Anthony Carter hooked up for the climactic play. The score was tied 21–21, and Indiana coach Lee Corso was happy about the fact that he was coming into Michigan Stadium and was walking out with a tie.

With six seconds left, Michigan pushed the ball toward midfield. In a controversial call, Michigan running back Lawrence Reid fumbled the football out of bounds and into the hands of Coach Corso. Corso held onto the ball and argued it had been deliberately thrown out of bounds to stop the clock. "I thought it was a clean fumble from where I was standing on the sidelines," Falk said.

Obviously, Corso didn't see it that way.

On the next play, Wangler dropped back in the pocket and fired the completion of the season to Carter. The speedster from Florida cut to the middle of the field and then completed the magic trick of the season by breaking tackles and reclaiming his balance just when it looked like he was going to fall. With no time left, Carter romped past the fallen Hoosiers into the end zone.

"Lee is a good friend of mine," Falk said. "And I still tease him about the whole play. I don't know what you were so upset about…you still made the second best catch of the game!"

1980

After the 1979 season, Bo had a vision to build the Midwest's first full-service indoor football facility, allowing college players to practice inside on a 100-yard long field. It was Bo's dream to practice in a facility in which he had full control. "I want to prepare myself and the team for the Rose Bowl," he said. "We go out to the Rose Bowl and spend 14 or 15 days out there practicing. With the indoor building, we can practice at our will, leave, and only be in California for seven days. And the kids won't be worn out when they get there. They will be nice and spry and willing to help Michigan win the game."

So the indoor building was built. One day standing next to Bo, Falk was watching his players practice. They could only pad three-quarters of the field. Bo said, "Why don't we have the whole indoors of these walls covered with padding? Why do we have to keep going one way all the time?"

Falk told him there was $90,000-plus in padding and that they didn't have enough money to pad the whole building. Bo was upset. "I'll tell you right now," Bo said "I don't believe that. That's terrible."

Suddenly Anthony Carter caught a pass on the sidelines, hit the padding on the wall, fell down, and hopped back up. Falk said, "There you go Bo. We just paid for those pads."

They both laughed, and Bo ordered the rest of the padding to be installed. That indoor building propelled Michigan to go to Pasadena and win Bo's first Rose Bowl game 23–6 against Washington. It marked the first time under Bo that Michigan had won the Rose Bowl.

1981

Just two games stick out in Jon Falk's mind for the 1981 season—the Wisconsin and Illinois contests. "Michigan had a veteran team and some great linemen in Ed Muransky and Bubba Paris," Falk said. "We thought for sure that we were going to have a great football team, but we stalled early."

Michigan was the preseason No. 1 college team in America when it traveled to Wisconsin. "We had a great tailback by the name of Butch Woolfolk," Falk said. "We struggled and lost 21–14. It wasn't the start that we had anticipated."

When a team loses that first game, it has to dig itself out of a hole. Later in the year, Michigan had to play Illinois, and the Fighting Illini also had a great team. At least the Wolverines thought they did. Illinois came to Michigan, thinking that this was its year to beat Michigan, and the Illini were up 21–7 at the end of the first quarter.

And then Michigan quarterback Steve Smith took them on a run that didn't end until the Wolverines said it was enough. Michigan took the ball into the end zone every time it touched the ball and wound up winning the game 70–21. Illinois wasn't going to win the Big Ten championship, and Michigan did end up going to play Ohio State for the championship.

1982

Sometimes a single critical play can cause a raucous stadium to resemble a silent cemetery. That's the way it was at Illinois, when Michigan stuffed the football down the Fighting Illini's throats on the last possession of the game. Michigan was leading 16–10 when Illinois got the ball with five minutes left in the game. Michigan kicker Ali Haji Sheik had already kicked field goals of 45 and 47 yards to give the Wolverines the six-point cushion.

But Illinois had a great quarterback in Tony Eason, who drove the Illini down the field with five minutes left in the game and with the ball sitting five yards away from the end zone.

That's when the crowd turned totally wild, and the Michigan defense challenged Illinois to give it all they had. On first down Eason threw a pass into the end zone that was dropped. On third down Eason connected for three yards that took the ball to the two-yard line.

On the last call of the game, running back Dwight Beverly tried a run up the right side. But Carlton Rose was waiting, and the rest of the Michigan defense stood tall to stop him at the one-yard line. Michigan walked off the field a 16–10 winner, and the earlier screams and cheers turned silent. "I never heard such a racket in the stadium that disappeared so quickly," Falk said. "I'll never forget that one."

1983

Any victory over Ohio State is a sweet one, but the 1983 game was special. Michigan jumped out to a 10–0 lead against the Buckeyes, and everyone knew that the winner was going to the Sugar Bowl. Quarterback Steve Smith carried the ball with exceptional flair that day as Michigan hammered Ohio State 24–21.

A key moment was when Earle Bruce attempted a bit of trickery. He tried to replicate the fumblerooski play Nebraska successfully used in a game against Oklahoma in 1979. The play was designed for the quarterback to fake receiving the snap, but the center instead places the ball down, and the left guard picks it up to rush. However, backup guard Jim Lachey never got his hands on the ball, and Michigan defensive tackle Nate Rodgers crashed center Joe Dooley. Michigan lineman Mike Hammerstein recovered the ball.

1984

As the Detroit Tigers were busy winning a World Series that year, Jim Harbaugh was equally busy carving out one of the finest seasons for a Michigan quarterback. Michigan opened the season at home against the preseason No. 1 pick Miami. None of the so-called experts gave Michigan a chance to win, but Harbaugh stole the spotlight from celebrated Miami quarterback Bernie Kosar in a 22–14 Michigan victory.

Things seemed upbeat for the Wolverines, even though they had such a young quarterback. But that good time ended with the sudden crack of Harbaugh's right throwing arm.

What turned the whole season sour was the game when Harbaugh got knocked out of the rest of the season against Michigan State. He suffered a broken right arm while diving to make a fumble recovery. With Harbaugh out the season had a nightmarish end.

Many in the media said that Michigan was finished. They kept harping that Michigan had a "Model T Ford offense" and weren't modern enough to win again in the Big Ten. Bo preached to the players to let the newspapers keep writing and babbling. The Wolverines already were planning their comeback. And they wouldn't forget.

Michigan finished 6–6 that year and lost to Brigham Young, the eventual national champion, in the Holiday Bowl. But Harbaugh would be back and healthy in 1985.

1985

The Wolverines drove their "Model T Ford" offense into Iowa on October 19 along with their No. 2 national ranking, and Iowa was ranked No. 1. It marked just the 19th time in history that the top two teams met in a showdown.

Quarterback Jim Harbaugh celebrates the game-winning touchdown pass he threw to John Kolesar against Ohio State in 1985. (Courtesy University of Michigan Athletic Department)

It was a great football game to watch, but Michigan wound up losing 12–10 in a bruising game by both teams.

Iowa Coach Hayden Fry had the visitors' locker room painted in pink. It was designed to make the visitors feel docile. Although the Hawkeyes won, the action was anything but docile on the field. Both teams tried to outslug the other in a well-played game.

Bo ordered Jon Falk to make the locker room white. So he had to buy yards and yards of butcher paper to paste to the wall. "Bo had his own idea," Falk said. "He ordered me to go out on Friday and cover the locker room with white paper. We covered the locker room upstairs and the halftime room with white paper. At the end of the day, it didn't make any difference because Michigan played hard that afternoon, and we should have won, but Iowa kicked a field goal with seconds left in the game, and we lost 12–10."

Another memorable moment occurred against Ohio State. The Buckeyes had narrowed the score to 20–17 on a 36-yard touchdown from from Jim Karsatos to Cris Carter. But Jim Harbaugh came up clutch with a huge fourth-quarter play to seal the victory. The Wolverines quarterback and future head coach threw a 77-yard touchdown to John Kolesar. Part of Harbaugh's 16-of-19, 230-yard, three-touchdown passing day, that play not only clinched Michigan's 27–17 victory against its rival Ohio State, but it also steered the Wolverines to the Fiesta Bowl.

1986

After being the No. 2 team in the country, Michigan lost at home 20–17 to Minnesota. Bo was going for his 166th win at Michigan to claim the top spot. Jon Falk had an engraved plaque ready to celebrate the honor. It would have to wait as Jim Harbaugh gave everyone else something to think about.

He guaranteed that Michigan was going to beat Ohio State at Columbus the following week. "I remember Bo rolling his eyes when I told him what Jimmy had said to the media in the locker room," Falk said, laughing. "At least he didn't say we were going to lose."

Jim Harbaugh, who made the famous guarantee in 1986, stands in between fellow Michigan Men, Jim Brandstatter (left) and Jon Falk (right).

Harbaugh got the last laugh and put tears in the Buckeyes' eyes when Michigan held on for a 26–24 victory on its way to the Rose Bowl. The victory gave Michigan its first Rose Bowl berth since 1982. It was the 32nd Big Ten title for Michigan, and the victory made Bo the winningest coach in Michigan history. "I never saw a player get harassed more than Jimmy did throughout that whole game," Falk said. "But Jimmy was always a tough kid—physically and mentally. He loved to be challenged. He refused to be intimidated. He prevailed and wound up as one of Michigan's finest quarterbacks in history."

1987

Three distinct memories from 1987 will always stay with Jon Falk. First was the game at Minnesota. Bo and Jon were standing at the sidelines when Minnesota was down at its own 2-yard line. Minnesota tailback Darrell Thompson broke out and was headed down Michigan's sideline all by himself for a 98-yard touchdown. As he ran past the Michigan bench, there was no one near him on the field. "I looked up at Bo and raised my right leg and teased Bo that I was going to trip him as he ran past us," Falk said.

"I'd like to do it myself, but just let him go," Bo said as Thompson ran past them. He took it the whole 98 yards for a touchdown.

At Illinois the one play that stands out in Jon's mind is Phil Webb going around the left side for two yards and scoring the touchdown in a come-from-behind 17–14 win, which pushed Michigan into the Hall of Fame Bowl to play Alabama. In that game John Kolesar caught a 20-yard pass into the end zone as time expired, and Michigan beat Alabama 28–24.

A separate memory away from the field is a happy one from a very tense time. Bo missed a game for the second time in his career because he had to be hospitalized for heart surgery. Fortunately, the surgery was successful, and the win over Alabama made Bo's recovery time a little smoother.

1988

The fate of the season always seems to come down to the last game against Ohio State, and it really doesn't matter if the game is in Ann Arbor or Columbus. Jon Falk received a lot of calls from friends in Ohio during the week before the annual clash. "They kept telling me how bad Ohio State was and how they expected Michigan to clobber the Buckeyes." Falk said. "Well, you never clobber Ohio State in Columbus, but I've got to admit I was feeling pretty good with the 20–0 score we had posted in the first half. I thought maybe my friends were right. We are better than Ohio State."

But then the second half came around, and the picture began to take a different shape. Ohio State scored 14 points in the third quarter. It jumped up on Michigan 31–27 with two minutes left in the game. Michigan never stopped Ohio State from scoring a touchdown in each one of their drives in the second half.

Then John Kolesar took it upon himself to turn things around after Ohio State had scored to pull ahead. Kolesar returned a kickoff 59 yards, leaving 41 yards from the goal line and victory. Michigan had one incomplete pass, and then Demetrius Brown took the next snap, faked a pass, dodged the tackler, and lofted the ball high into the end zone on the left side where

Kolesar eluded two Ohio State defenders to reach up and catch the ball at the goal line and fall into the end zone. Michigan went ahead 34–31. Ohio State had one more chance. The Buckeyes drove down to the Michigan 40-yard line, and then Marc Spencer intercepted a pass. It was the only drive in the second half that the Buckeyes didn't score.

Michigan beat Ohio State 34–31. That propelled the Wolverines into the Rose Bowl, and they ended up defeating USC 22–14. It was Bo's second Rose Bowl win.

1989

The most memorable game that year was against Michigan State at East Lansing. Michigan had a good football team in 1989 and so did MSU. Michigan was up 10–0, but MSU had a fourth-and-goal play right at the beginning of the fourth quarter. MSU coach George Perles decided to go for a touchdown in a 10–0 game.

On the 17th play of the drive, the Spartans handed the ball off to the out-standing running back Blake Ezor, who got smothered by the defensive line just short of the goal line. Probably in retrospect, Tripp Wellborne's hit was the first and perhaps most important play for the Wolverines in 1989 because it propelled Michigan to the Big Ten championship. It defeated Ohio State that year, which was Bo's last game against the Buckeyes as head football coach.

No Michigan fan will ever forget the hard-fought 1990 Rose Bowl against USC. It was the battle of two bruising defenses. In the fourth quarter, there was a gigantic turning point. On fourth-and-2 at the Michigan 46-yard line, Bo called for Chris Stapleton to fake a punt.

Stapleton ran the play beautifully and took it 24 yards for the first down. But elation quickly switched to frustration. Michigan was hit with a holding penalty and an unsportsmanlike conduct penalty. Bo couldn't believe that a holding penalty was called. In his mad dash to catch one of the referees, Bo's legs and arms got caught up in all the cords that the team had on the sidelines, and he went down—*hard*.

Former Michigan coach Gary Moeller, who also coached in the NFL, calls Big Jon the best equipment manager he ever had.

That's really the way the season ended. So the most memorable thing about Bo's last game at Michigan was that he was tripped by a telephone line during a 17–10 loss in the Rose Bowl.

1990

Bo picked assistant Gary Moeller to succeed him as the head coach. Mo was the right man. He shared a lot of Bo's philosophies with several of his own. He was an outstanding recruiter and basically ran Bo's offense with a little more passing to keep opponents off stride. Bo was satisfied with his selection as head coach and expected big things out of Mo.

Heisman Trophy winner Desmond Howard makes an acrobatic catch against Notre Dame.
(Courtesy University of Michigan Athletic Department)

But it was a tough year for Michigan because it started out with a couple of difficult games—Michigan State and Iowa at home. Nobody will ever forget the MSU game. In a 28–27 game with no time left, Elvis Grbac dropped back and was looking for All-American wide receiver Desmond Howard. Grbac spotted him and threw that ball at Howard, who tripped as he went into the end zone and dropped the pass. The ball fell to the ground, and in a controversial decision, the game was declared over with Michigan State up by one point. The interesting story behind that is Eddie Brown was the defensive back who was involved in the play. "I met him a few years later," Jon Falk said. "I said, 'You're the man who interfered with Desmond Howard in the end zone in 1990.'" Brown laughed and said it was simply a matter of good defense. "We both laughed about it," Falk said. "And as we shook hands, I said, 'Please be careful not to trip me as you walk by me.'"

1991

The game that everyone remembers is the Ohio State-Michigan contest when Desmond Howard caught a punt on Michigan's own 7-yard line and ran the ball back 93 yards for a touchdown. It was the longest punt return in Michigan history and Howard capped the moment by breaking into his Heisman Trophy pose. The fans in The Big House went wild and so did the commentators. Announcer Keith Jackson aptly said, "Good-bye Ohio State, hello Heisman."

1992

"Three things in particular about the 1992 season always stick in my memory," Jon Falk said. First is the 22–22 tie against Illinois. After coming off that tie, Michigan had to go to Columbus to play Ohio State. The Buckeyes scored 10 points in the fourth quarter and tied the game 13–13. The Ohio State athletic director strangely dubbed that tie, which was actually Michigan's third tie that year, as "one of our greatest wins ever."

Michigan played Washington again in the Rose Bowl. The Wolverines lost to the Huskies 34–14 the year before in the Rose Bowl. Mo made it a point that Michigan's objective was to sing "The Victors" in Pasadena. And the players kept that in their minds and hearts. Michigan ended up beating Washington 38–31 for Mo's Rose Bowl victory.

Tyrone Wheatley, now a Michigan coach, was the MVP. He had a record-breaking 88-yard touchdown run and was clearly the best player on the field. In the locker room after the game, the team indeed sang "The Victors."

1993

What Michigan faced at Wisconsin was nothing short of mayhem. The Badgers primed themselves for the upset and completed their mission with a 13–10 victory. After time expired hundreds of out-of-control fans jumped the fences and charged the field in a frightening sight that looked more like it belonged in a third-world country.

They rushed the field and had to dance around fallen bodies in an out-of-control celebration. "I'll never forget this," Jon Falk said. "We heard sirens up in the locker room and wondered what was going on. When I tried to cross the field to get to the locker room, it looked like a battleground. Bodies laying all over. The fences were torn down. When the people stormed the field, they pushed people out of the way. They pushed the fence surrounding the stadium on the people. I saw people with broken arms, broken legs. Faces looked like they had been put on a grill. That was a very disheartening feeling. But Coach Moeller was able to rebound from that ugly feeling to prepare for the rest of the season."

Ohio State was undefeated and the fifth-ranked team in the country. Because the Buckeyes already had clinched the Big Ten championship, the championship trophy was sent to Michigan so that the school could give it to Ohio State after playing their final game. So on Friday, when Ohio State was working out, Falk put the trophy in front of the locker room door and said: "Hey, here's the trophy you guys won…you know you already won the Big Ten championship."

As the players were walking out, they all grabbed the trophy. They looked at it and the coaches looked at it. Falk kind of laughed to himself, thinking that if Michigan had faced the same situation, *Bo or Mo would have said to "take that trophy away, we've done nothing until we beat Ohio State."*

"Maybe because we had won a bunch of championships in a row, they were starving for satisfaction," Falk said. He ran quickly to the office where Mo was preparing for the Friday afternoon practice. "Coach," Falk began excitedly, "tomorrow will be like feeding grain to crappies because Ohio State is not ready to play Michigan."

"I don't know," he said. "I don't think it's going to be that easy, but I hope you're right."

"We ended up winning that game 28–0," Falk said. "It was 21–0 at the end of the first half, and I saw the eyes of the Ohio players when they came off that field. They looked like they had just walked out of *The Wizard of Oz,* and I knew then that we had beaten Ohio State." Michigan went on to win the Hall of Fame Bowl against North Carolina State 42–7.

1994

Two non-conference games stood out in the 1994 season. The first was a 26–24 victory at Notre Dame. The second is a still-hard-to-believe last-second loss to Colorado in The Big House. At Notre Dame the Fighting Irish had just pulled ahead 24–23 with 46 seconds left in the game. Michigan got the ball on the 16-yard line. With Todd Collins at quarterback, Michigan began to move the ball downfield. "As we kept advancing the ball, kicker Remy Hamilton came over to me and asked where the kicking net was," Jon Falk said. "I looked around and I spotted one of my assistants had taken the kicking net and was heading down to the locker room. I ran out to try to yell at him, but the crowd was so loud, and he was so worried about getting to the locker room that the kicking net went off into the sunset. I looked at Remy and said, 'You're going to have to practice without the ball.' So he was just kicking his leg into the wind to practice to kick a 42-yard field goal."

And it worked. He kicked a clean 42-yarder, and Michigan won 26–24. "Remy never lets me forget the fact that one of my boys had taken the net away," Falk chuckled. "I tell him to look at it this way: you had less time to worry about it."

Then, of course, the game that will always stand out and added a whole new dimension to the term "Hail Mary pass" was the one thrown by Colorado with no time remaining on the clock. It truly was demoralizing to the whole Michigan team. Colorado had a great team that year. Former Michigan assistant Bill McCartney was the head coach. Elliot Uzelac, another former Michigan assistant, was an assistant at Colorado.

With two minutes left in the game, Michigan clung to a 26–21 lead. Michigan was unable to run out the clock, and Colorado got the ball back on the 15-yard line with 15 seconds left. Kordell Stewart dropped back and threw a pass up into the end zone that was close to 70 yards in the air. "As we stood on the sidelines, we watched the ball go up, and it looked to me like it was getting ready to tilt at the 20-yard line and fall down," Falk said. "All of a sudden something lifted that ball up in the air and took it into the end zone and it fell into the hands of the enemy. The game was over, and they won 27–26."

The entire Colorado team swarmed the field yelling and screaming. Falk went into the Colorado locker room to congratulate McCartney, a very religious man, who said that, "The Lord was on our side today."

Falk shook his friend's hand and replied, "That was just a long pass that a man caught that won the game today, Bill."

1995

The Lloyd Carr era officially started with the Fall Classic. Virginia was in town to play the Wolverines, and the result couldn't have been more thrilling.

Virginia was up 17–11. Michigan then launched a 16-play drive. With no time on the clock, receiver Mercury Hayes went into the end zone and caught a ball that Scott Dreisbach just lofted into the right-hand corner of the end zone. Hayes was able to get one foot down in the end zone. All the Michigan players shot their arms to the sky after the dramatic victory, and Carr smiled warmly. He put his hands up, indicating that a touchdown had been scored. The 18–17 victory was a preview of good things to come under Carr.

The other unforgettable game that year came at home when Tim Biakabutuka rambled for 313 yards rushing, and Michigan beat Eddie George and Ohio State 31–23. "I saw Eddie George at the Rose Bowl a few years later," Jon Falk recalled. "I said, 'How about that 1995 team?' He looked up at me and said, 'The 1995 game makes my heart hurt every time I think about that. I guess you have to say that anyone from Ohio State has to hate Michigan. I'll tell you one thing, though, I love to watch Michigan play.'"

Falk smiled and put his arm around George. "You know what?" Falk said with the wink of his eye. "I love to watch Ohio State play, too."

1996

Ohio State was undefeated when Michigan went to Columbus. The Buckeyes probably had one of the best teams in the country, but Michigan was able to hold them to nine points in the first half. The Buckeyes were inside the Michigan 10-yard line three times and had to settle for three field goals.

Right before the second half, quarterback Scott Dreisbach got hurt and was replaced by Brian Griese. In the first minute of the second half, Griese threw a quick pass to Tai Streets, who ran a slant pattern toward the middle of the field. Ohio State's Shawn Springs lost his footing and slipped, allowing Streets to run 69 yards for a touchdown in the first minute of the second half. That play silenced the stunned Ohio State crowd. "I remember standing on the sidelines and staring at Shawn Springs and the entire defensive backfield," Jon Falk said. "I kept telling them: 'This is Michigan you're playing…this is Michigan…just remember who you're playing. We are Michigan.'"

Michigan pulled ahead 10–9 on a Hamilton field goal. Then he kicked another field goal to make it 13–9, a result Falk kind of predicted. "I told kicker Remy Hamilton the Thursday before we left that if he kicked a field goal to beat Ohio State that I'm going to get you a T-shirt and it's going say 'I won the Ohio State game.'"

"I can't even tell everyone how proud I was of our entire team that day," Falk said. "A great coaching job, a great performance by the kids, and a great 13–9 victory for the University of Michigan."

After the game Falk walked up to Hamilton and told him he would have that T-shirt the next day. "Every time I see Remy to this day, he always laughs and says he still has that T-shirt," Falk recalled.

1997

It's tough to explain a miracle. But for sure it demands blind commitment and a singular goal to win. The 1997 Michigan team was relentless in its pursuit of excellence and confident in its faith in each other.

Michigan's most recent champtionship team poses in front of the Rose Bowl.

Michigan won the Big Ten, the national championship, and went undefeated. And Jon Falk believes firmly that unbeatable spirit started with quarterback Brian Griese, who wasn't even sure he would be the starter in the spring long before spring camp began.

Falk got a feeling that something special was going to happen when Griese visited his office after the quarterback had talked to coach Lloyd Carr. Griese was a fifth-year senior and needed only a couple of classes to graduate. He went to talk to Carr about returning for his fifth year. After telling Carr it was his intention to return for one more year, Griese stopped into Falk's office to tell him what he had decided. "What are you doing that for, Brian?" Falk asked. "You can leave with a University of Michigan degree in your back pocket and you can get a good job. Why would you want to come back?"

Griese was quick with his response. "Because I want to go to the Rose Bowl," he said.

Of course, everyone is familiar with the results as Griese became the true leader of the team. "That was a tough, talented, and close team," Falk said. "Of all the teams I've been on at Michigan, that was what you would call a team because nobody cared who scored a touchdown, nobody cared who got the tackle. The goal that year when the seniors got together at the beginning of the year was just win. And that's what we did. We just won every football game that we played."

1998

"We got fooled," Jon Falk said. "Or maybe we let ourselves get fooled."

But coming off the 1997 season and beating Ohio State and winning the Rose Bowl and the national championship, everybody on the team thought that 1998 was going to pick up where 1997 left off. "Everybody was going to play together," Falk continued, "the chips were going to fall our way, and we would just keep on winning from start to finish."

But that's not what happened. The season started a little rougher than anticipated. Notre Dame beat Michigan 36–20.

And in one of the most impressive games Falk has ever seen by an opponent at Michigan Stadium, the Wolverines were humbled. That incredible performance came from Syracuse quarterback Donovan McNabb. He shot Syracuse to a 17–0 first-quarter lead and then stretched it to 24–0 before Michigan scored in the first half.

Syracuse scored 14 more points in the third quarter to finish the game with a 38–28 rout.

Jon Jansen was the captain of the team and knew he had to take another step forward to help turn the team around. "I said a few words to Jon after the game to help in any way I could," Falk said. "'I'm afraid that the guys on this team still think it's 1997 and I think we have to go around saying, *This is our team, this is the 1998 team…not the 1997 team anymore.*'"

So Jansen had a team meeting that night and explained what was happening to the players. The next week Michigan beat Eastern Michigan, but there was another matter to settle. Michigan had a pair of incredibly talented quarterbacks—Tom Brady and Drew Henson. Both were battling to start.

Falk took Brady aside. "Tom, I know you're upset because you're not starting," Falk said. "But you're the leader on this team, and if we're going to win the Big Ten championship, you're going to have to show these players that it's not bothering you. The way you act is the way this team is going to act. Tom looked at me and said he had been wanting to talk to somebody about this situation for a long time."

"I know that I can start for this team," Brady said. " I know that I can get this team to win."

Falk slapped Brady on the back. "Then keep your mouth shut and don't complain," Falk said. "Go out and just play football and hold this team together. You're the leader on this team."

Brady started the game at Michigan State and never relinquished another start. Michigan won the Big Ten championship thanks to the leadership of Jansen and Brady.

1999

The following year Tom Brady played the best football of his life. In similar fashion to the way Brady perfected late rallies for the New England Patriots, he guided the Wolverines. Late in the fourth quarter at Penn State, Brady scored on a five-yard run. With 1:46 left in the game, he fired a game-clinching touchdown pass to complete the victory.

The following week Michigan beat Ohio State 24–17, and the Wolverines were selected to play Alabama in the 2000 Orange Bowl. Alabama had the electrifying Shaun Alexander running the ball and had a terrific first half. In the second half, however, Brady and wide receiver David Terrell played pitch and catch all over the field to send the game into overtime. "I'll always remember standing next to Coach Carr when the Alabama kicker sliced the attempt for a game-tying extra point in overtime that would have extended the game even longer," Falk said. "I slapped Lloyd on the back and shouted,

'They missed the kick.' Lloyd looked at me and said, 'How about that…we just beat Alabama.'"

2000

Three familiar foes made for three exciting games that year. During a great defensive battle with Michigan State, Michigan scored one touchdown in the first half and another in the second for a 14–0 shutout. The best defensive play was turned in by Larry Foote.

Michigan State fumbled away the football, and Foote charged from a handful of Spartans to dive and keep the ball from going out of bounds. We recovered that fumble off their drive and ended up winning by a pair of hard-fought touchdowns.

The game at Northwestern didn't feature much defense. The Wildcats wound up winning 54–51 in a never-ending point parade. The play that decided the game came with only seconds left when Anthony Thomas fumbled the ball on the 25-yard line. He had broken through the line, and there was nothing left between him and the goal line 75 yards away when the ball slipped from his hands, and Northwestern recovered. "I really felt bad for Anthony Thomas," Jon Falk said. "He was one of the best tailbacks in the history of Michigan football and a tremendous human being."

The other vivid memory in Falk's mind from that season was watching Drew Henson's magic spring to life at Ohio Stadium. Henson threw a pass across the field into the end zone. It covered the whole width of the field, and David Terrell caught it in the end zone. "I bet it carried 65 yards in the air," Falk said. "I'd never seen anything like that before."

Michigan got the ball back, and Henson put on another offensive show. He dropped back and ran one yard for the touchdown on a fourth-down keeper. He faked inside and then ran to the left to score. And then the celebration began as the Wolverines won 38–26.

Henson was an incredible all-around athlete who performed his magic on the biggest sports stages in America. He played for the New York Yankees, the

Dallas Cowboys, and the Detroit Lions. A few years after he turned pro, Henson returned to Ann Arbor and was asked by Falk what his greatest sports thrill was. With hardly any hesitation, Henson said it was the game in Columbus when he led Michigan to victory over the Buckeyes in the Horseshoe.

2001

In Jon Falk's mind, the Michigan State game that year should be entered into the record books with an asterisk next to the final score. After all, how often does a home team get an extra second to run an extra play after time has expired?

That's what it looked like when Spartans quarterback Jeff Smoker spiked the ball with no time left. Falk looked at the clock and started running off the field. He tucked his hat tightly on his head so it wouldn't fall off as he was running into the locker room. He turned his head, and all of a sudden, there were two seconds left on the clock. How can that be? Smoker spiked the ball, and the clock stopped with two seconds left in the game. They were able to throw the ball into the end zone and beat Michigan 26–24.

That was the first time in Falk's life that he was running off the field feeling sure he had won—only to see that the clock had stopped. As Michigan fans found out, the timekeeper at the time was called "Spartan Bob" for his strong affinity for the Spartans. The next year the Big Ten changed the rule and made one of the field officials responsible for keeping time.

Then Michigan played Wisconsin before one of the most raucous crowds anywhere in the country. It probably compares to the atmosphere at Ohio State. In a 17–17 game, Michigan was forced to punt the ball with less than 30 seconds left. Hayden Epstein punted the ball. The ball bounced sideways and hit the back of a Wisconsin player, and Brandon Williams, one of Michigan's rushers, grabbed the ball on the 13-yard line and covered it. Michigan kicked a field goal with six seconds left in the game for the victory. "As I was running off the field," Falk said, "I laughed to myself and said, *That's how you win at Wisconsin.*"

2002

Michigan hosted Wisconsin in one of the hardest-fought football games Jon Falk had seen. "We ended up beating Wisconsin 21–14," Falk said. "While we were celebrating the win, the equipment manager for Wisconsin came across the hall to tell me the showers in the visitors' locker room were cold. I immediately went to check out the problem so that we could deliver the same sort of courtesy we always received on the road."

Athletic director Bill Martin and Falk stood outside the shower room and apologized to every player as they left the cold showers. While coach Barry Alvarez badgered Falk, his longtime friend, saying he struggled to understand why Michigan "can't afford to have hot water in a stadium where they draw over 100,000 people."

"The locker rooms were old," Falk said, "and he was pretty sure that Fielding Yost used that locker room over there in the corner."

From that day forward at Michigan Stadium, they made sure that the showers were turned on in the visitors' locker room with five minutes left in the game. "Now whenever Coach Alvarez and I meet, we shake hands and laugh at the situation," Falk said. "He's an outstanding leader who really cares about the athletes in all of Wisconsin sports. He's a good friend."

2003

Jon Falk knows the kind of leader John Navarre was. "I can still hear the voice of quarterback John Navarre when he spoke to the team in the locker room after the game at Michigan State," Falk said. Navarre said: "Men, I'm going to ask you to dedicate yourselves for the next two weeks to beat Northwestern and to come back and beat Ohio State for the Big Ten championship," he said. "I want this championship real bad for Michigan and I promise you this: I will play the best you will ever see John Navarre play and I'm asking you to do the same thing."

The speech by Navarre came after running back Chris Perry, also one of the toughest guys on the team, turned in one of the most electrifying performances in the history of the battle for the Paul Bunyan Trophy. Perry carried the ball 51 times for 219 yards in a 27–20 Michigan victory. Perry was one of the toughest guys on the team, Falk said.

Bo watched the game on television at his home. Falk went to see him after getting the equipment unloaded. "Jon, I love that game," Bo looked up toward his friend. "Fifty-one carries. That's the way football is played right there. That is what Michigan football is all about."

Three weeks later against Ohio State, Perry registered another performance that delighted the crowd in Michigan Stadium. He ran the ball for 154 yards on 31 carries and scored two touchdowns in a 35–21 Michigan victory. That was the 100th game between Michigan and Ohio State.

2004

What started as a day game turned into a night game. What started as an embarrassing Michigan Stadium loss turned into one of the most exciting victories in Wolverine history. Trailing 27–10 with eight minutes left in the game, Michigan staged a magical triple-overtime victory that will be remembered by both sides forever.

The Paul Bunyan Trophy, of course, is always at stake when Michigan plays Michigan State. The equipment manager at Michigan State and Falk have an agreement that ensures the winning team gets the trophy at the end of the game. So with the score 27–10, Jon Falk walked across the field to assure his counterpart he'd have the Trophy "ready for you" at the end of the game. "Don't you think you're a little premature?" the Spartans equipment manager said.

"Twenty-seven to 10," Falk said. "That's a little bit too much without enough time to do it."

After an onside kick, though, suddenly the race for the finish was on. Following three overtimes the Wolverines turned tragedy into opportunity for a 45–37 victory. "I remember Lloyd saying that this game speaks to the spirit of the stadium and to the tradition of this rivalry," Falk said. "Anybody

Big Jon took meticulous care of the Little Brown Jug given to the winner of the Michigan-Minnesota game, college football's oldest rivalry.

who watched this game either in the stadium or on TV across this country will say they saw one of the greatest games in football history."

2005

It's always tough to lose a rivalry game like the one for the Little Brown Jug. Jon Falk's stomach still gets a little upset when looking back at the 2005 loss. Falk and former Minnesota coach Glen Mason are good friends. The pair still talk about that Minnesota upset whenever they get together. "I used to get Glen a cup of coffee before each game in Michigan," Falk said. "He's a good friend and a good person. I remember him coming over because he wanted to know if there really is a Little Brown Jug."

Minnesota hadn't seen that little brown beauty since 1986. "How do I even know it exists?" Mason said with a smile.

"Glen," Falk said. "It really does exist. I've got it locked up. I hope you never do see it, but maybe someday you might."

In that 2005 game with only seconds left and the score tied 20–20, the clock malfunctioned. No one really knew how much time was left when a Minnesota running back broke for a 61-yard run. The Gophers quickly got into position and kicked a field goal for a three-point victory. Those Gopher players ran across that field and grabbed that jug out of Falk's hand. "I'll never forget that feeling," Falk said "but after the game I went in to see Mason and said, 'Congratulations, you won the Little Brown Jug. You played Ohio State tough and you beat them. You played us tough the last two years, and we were lucky to win. Today you got the upper hand, but I'm promising you this—next year we're coming back and we're getting that little brown beauty back to us. Take care of it and don't break it.'"

Mason told Falk that back in Minnesota he and his wife went out to dinner. They were in the car, and he had the Little Brown Jug in his hand. She said just leave the jug in the car. "Are you kidding me?" Mason said. "If somebody takes this Little Brown Jug, I've got to face Jon Falk. And I'm not going to do that."

Bo Schembechler passed away in 2006, but Cheri Falk (left) and Jon remain close with Bo's widow, Cathy (middle).

So he took the Little Brown Jug with him into the restaurant, and the next thing you know, there was a line of people standing there wanting to touch and look at the precious little thing.

2006

Michigan fans throughout the nation remember the 2006 season because that's when Bo died, which was perhaps ironically the day before the Ohio State game. "Losing Bo as a man was far more painful than losing a former Michigan football coach," Jon Falk said. "Bo was iconic to Michigan fans, the state of Michigan, and the whole world of sports. I remember Ohio State students walking by when we were unloading the equipment truck. They saw the tears in my eyes, and some said they would say a prayer for our loss. He was my best friend."

One of the most memorable moments from that season was playing Ball State. It was a non-conference game, which was unusual that late in the schedule. Former Michigan assistant coach Brady Hoke was the head coach at Ball State. It also was the week that Bo had to go to the hospital to get his pacemaker for his heart adjusted. Falk had the opportunity to talk to Hoke before the game. Everyone was concerned about Bo at the time.

Ball State came back after Michigan took the lead and kept fighting. The only way Michigan kept the lead was that Ryan Mundy intercepted a pass on a heave with time running out to preserve the 34–26 victory. "As soon as the game was over and we cleaned the locker room and got the equipment back over to Schembechler Hall, I went up to the hospital to see Bo," Falk said. "I walked into his room, and he was laying there. The first thing he did was grab my arm and said, 'Do you realize Brady Hoke almost beat us today? That son of a gun almost beat Michigan in Michigan Stadium. That was a well-coached team that we played today.'"

Falk said that scene in the hospital will live with him forever. "In fact, that whole season will," he said.

On Thursday before the Ohio State game, Bo addressed the team in Schembechler Hall. Sitting in on the uplifting speech were Falk and former strength and conditioning coach Mike Gittleson. Bo's fiery and tender words captured all the senses of everyone in the room. Gittleson and Falk were moved by Bo's passionate message. They told the old coach he had outdone himself. Everyone in the room couldn't have been moved any more.

Bo stared both in the eye. "You guys aren't kidding me, are you?" Bo demanded.

"That was a great talk, Coach," both replied. "We aren't trying to fool you."

Bo smiled and said he was glad. "Those were the last words I spoke to Bo," Falk said. "And I'll never forget that as long as I live."

On Friday morning when Falk was unloading the truck, he received a phone call from recruiting secretary Mary Passink telling Falk that Bo had just died. Students and passers-by expressed their condolences to the Michigan staff that was unloading the truck. They, too, understood the severity of the loss for college football.

2007

There were several shining games in 2007. The Illinois and Michigan State games truly show how much guts quarterback Chad Henne really has. Henne and Rick Leach are the only four-year starting quarterbacks to ever to play at Michigan as freshmen.

Against Illinois, Michigan fell behind, and Henne hurt his shoulder. "His arm dropped so low I thought it was going to fall down to the ground," Jon Falk said. Nevertheless, he forced himself back and threw a touchdown pass to Adrian Arrington. Michigan finished with a 27–17 victory. "I'll never forget how much pain Henne suffered, but I do know he put a whole new definition into a shoulder injury," Falk said.

Later at Michigan State, Henne ignored the aching shoulder by leading Michigan to 14 unanswered points in the fourth quarter in a 28–24 victory. Henne threw the touchdown pass to win the game. "Those were two of the gutsiest performances I had ever seen," Falk said.

In the Capital One Bowl, Michigan played Florida, and Henne had time to recover from injury. It also was Lloyd Carr's last game at Michigan. All the critics talked about before the game was the fact that Florida was bigger and faster and stronger than Michigan. The bookies predicted Michigan was coming to Florida for the slaughter of the Wolverines.

But a complete team effort knocked off the Gators 41–35. Carr was carried off the field on his players' shoulders, and a new era in Michigan was about to begin.

2008

It was a new coach in a whole new era. Rich Rodriguez, one of the nation's hot young coaches, brought his spread offense to Ann Arbor. But uneasiness accompanied the chasm of change, and RichRod survived only three years.

Michigan was beaten by Michigan State, and the Paul Bunyan Trophy was headed for East Lansing. "We had a tradition at both schools that the winning of Paul would always be celebrated in the winning locker room,"

Jon Falk said. "But before the game, the MSU equipment manager informed me that if MSU won, they wanted the trophy presentation on the field. It's something Michigan would never do, but it would be their choice. It hurt to see Paul go."

To this day MSU takes Paul onto the field after it wins. Michigan continues to have Paul in the locker room after a Michigan win. It was the first time in seven years that the Spartans won the intrastate rivalry game. Michigan State outplayed Michigan that year, and the Spartans deserved the trophy.

The most memorable game of 2008 was at Minnesota. The Gophers were having a good year, but Michigan wound up with the Little Brown Jug. Quarterback Nick Sheridan turned in one of the most gutsy performances on the road that season. Running the spread offense, Sheridan led the Wolverines to a 29–6 victory.

2009

Michigan started out with Western Michigan and then played Notre Dame at home. The Wolverines had a young freshman quarterback, Tate Forcier, and they battled Notre Dame right to the end.

Wide receiver Greg Mathews caught a pass with 11 seconds left, and Michigan beat the Fighting Irish. Everyone thought that Michigan was going to be able to slip out of the doldrums and get back to its winning ways in 2009. The Wolverines won the first four games, but they lost to Michigan State in overtime. "I think the most dramatic moment was when we played Ohio State in the last game of the year and we got beat," Jon Falk said. "But we had a linebacker by the name of Brandon Graham who had a great game against Ohio State. What a first-class showing to see all those Ohio State players at the end of the game shaking Brandon Graham's hand and telling him what a great four years he had at Michigan…That just shows you the respect that Michigan and Ohio State have for each other."

2010

Sophomore Denard Robinson was the quarterback and put together a season-long highlight tape of spectacular plays after seeing limited action in his freshman year. "I don't think anybody ever knew that when Robinson started playing as a sophomore how great he was going to be in Michigan history," Jon Falk said.

Robinson led Michigan to a late touchdown against Notre Dame in a 28–24 victory. He was the ninth quarterback in college football history to gain more than 200 yards passing and 200 yards running in the same game. He also scored on an 87-yard touchdown scamper. That was the day on which former Michigan All-American Ron Kramer passed away. "On the sideline we felt that was a great tribute that Denard Robinson ran 87 yards for a touchdown against Notre Dame in memory of Kramer's No. 87 jersey," Falk said. "The touchdown run against Notre Dame was a little slice of destiny."

Another significant game in 2010 came against Illinois. "It was our sixth win of the season and lifted us into a bowl game for the first time in three seasons," Falk said. "It was a beauty, a triple-overtime and 67–65 thriller. We were starting to show a few good players that would help us in the future. Denard Robinson, Junior Hemingway, and Roy Roundtree were starting to shine in the passing game."

2011

The first night game in the history of The Big House took place. Michigan also had the first player to wear a legendary player's number. That was Junior Hemingway wearing No. 21, honoring Heisman Trophy winner Desmond Howard, who wore the number from 1988 through 1991. And the game certainly lived up to all of its hype. A last second 35–31 comeback victory against Notre Dame made all Wolverine players, former players, and fans proud of first-year coach Brady Hoke.

Hoke led the team to an 11–2 record, including a 23–20 overtime victory against Virginia Tech in the Sugar Bowl. It marked Michigan's first BCS game since 2006. "Everything just fell into place for Michigan that year," Jon Falk reflected. "At the Sugar Bowl in New Orleans, we were able to play Virginia Tech. It was a hard-fought game. Denard Robinson played another great game, and we were able to kick a field goal in overtime to win 23–20. We won our first BCS bowl since we had beaten Alabama back in 2000. It was a great win for Michigan.

"In 2011, the big game of the year was also playing Ohio State at Michigan," Falk added. "Michigan hadn't beat OSU since 2003 so it was a very big game for us. Denard Robinson, who was a junior quarterback, helped us come back and beat the Buckeyes, 40–34. It was my most memorable game for the season."

2012

Everything is bigger in Texas, including the new Cowboys Stadium. "You could hang out there for a week and never be spotted," Jon Falk said. "We opened the season there against an incredibly talented Alabama team. We lost 41–14, but it was a good experience for the entire team."

That Alabama team would go on to win the national championship. Meanwhile, Denard Robinson was wrapping up a historic career. He set a Big Ten career record for rushing yards for a quarterback with 4,495 yards. In addition to Robinson's production, what stood out to Falk was the Michigan State game, which Michigan hosted in The Big House. Michigan kicked a field goal from 38 yards out with five seconds left and won 12–10. More importantly, it was the first time Michigan had beaten Michigan State in five years. "We took Paul Bunyan back," Falk said. "What a sight to see in the locker room after Paul was being passed around to everyone. Plenty of snapshots were taken. It felt great to have Paul back where he belongs."

Though the Wolverines played in an exciting, back-and-forth Outback Bowl on January 1, they lost to South Carolina 33–28 on a touchdown pass with 11 seconds left.

2013

This year would represent the end of the line for Jon Falk. "Athletic director Dave Brandon and I agreed this would be my final year before I retired," Falk said. "Dave told me it would be my farewell tour across the country. Each game was more valuable to me than any other games in the time that I had been at Michigan. Each one meant something."

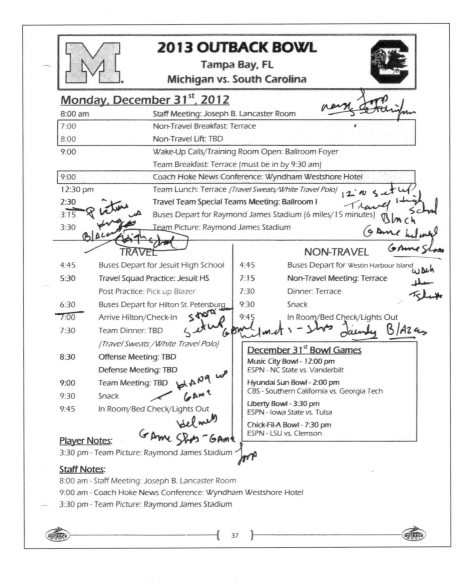

2013 OUTBACK BOWL
Tampa Bay, FL
Michigan vs. South Carolina

Monday, December 31st, 2012

8:00 am	Staff Meeting: Joseph B. Lancaster Room
7:00	Non-Travel Breakfast: Terrace
8:00	Non-Travel Lift: TBD
9:00	Wake-Up Calls/Training Room Open: Ballroom Foyer
	Team Breakfast: Terrace (must be in by 9:30 am)
9:00	Coach Hoke News Conference: Wyndham Westshore Hotel
12:30 pm	Team Lunch: Terrace *(Travel Sweats/White Travel Polo)*
2:30	Travel Team Special Teams Meeting: Ballroom I
3:15	Buses Depart for Raymond James Stadium (6 miles/15 minutes)
3:30	Team Picture: Raymond James Stadium

TRAVEL		NON-TRAVEL	
4:45	Buses Depart for Jesuit High School	4:45	Buses Depart for Westin Harbour Island
5:30	Travel Squad Practice: Jesuit HS	7:15	Non-Travel Meeting: Terrace
	Post Practice: Pick up Blazer	7:30	Dinner: Terrace
6:30	Buses Depart for Hilton St. Petersburg	9:30	Snack
7:00	Arrive Hilton/Check-In	9:45	In Room/Bed Check/Lights Out
7:30	Team Dinner: TBD		
	(Travel Sweats/White Travel Polo)		

December 31st Bowl Games

Music City Bowl - 12:00 pm
ESPN - NC State vs. Vanderbilt

Hyundai Sun Bowl - 2:00 pm
CBS - Southern California vs. Georgia Tech

Liberty Bowl - 3:30 pm
ESPN - Iowa State vs. Tulsa

Chick-Fil-A Bowl - 7:30 pm
ESPN - LSU vs. Clemson

8:30	Offense Meeting: TBD
	Defense Meeting: TBD
9:00	Team Meeting: TBD
9:30	Snack
9:45	In Room/Bed Check/Lights Out

Player Notes:
3:30 pm - Team Picture: Raymond James Stadium

Staff Notes:
8:00 am - Staff Meeting: Joseph B. Lancaster Room
9:00 am - Coach Hoke News Conference: Wyndham Westshore Hotel
3:30 pm - Team Picture: Raymond James Stadium

"We beat Notre Dame 41–30, and hopes were high that we were going to have a great year," Falk said. The victory was the 400th in the history of The Big House. Amazingly, Falk was busy at work for 209 of them.

"Then we went to Connecticut and I wound up missing the game," Falk said. "I was greeting the team at the locker room door and I tripped and fell in the hallway. I got up and couldn't catch my breath so I had to go into the locker room to sit down. Brandon walked in and saw me and thought I was having a heart attack. I was sitting in the cardiac care unit in East Hartford, Connecticut, during the game, and maybe that was a good place to be because we narrowly survived an upset and finally won 24–21. As it turns out, I was fine. I just had the wind knocked out of me."

"The Minnesota game was a homecoming game, and that was my last Little Brown Jug game," Falk said. "It was a tremendous feeling to be able to win the Little Brown Jug and carry it off the field. Before the Minnesota game Jil Gordon, who paints the scores on the jug, had a miniature jug to give me. It was a fine ending to my career against Minnesota with the win and the jug to carry off the field."

And there were still plenty of surprises to celebrate as the season rolled on. Northwestern gave Falk a game jersey when Michigan got to Evanston, Illinois. Michigan won that game 27–19 in triple overtime.

"I think the most memorable thing of the season was the week before the OSU game," Falk said. "Brady [Hoke] brought me up before the team and reminded them that this was my final home game." Hoke told his players that 40 years at any place is a tremendous accomplishment. At Michigan it's almost inconceivable. In front of the whole team, Hoke announced that he was making Falk an honorary captain for the OSU game. "That made me cry," Falk said. "I thanked Brady and the team and I remember walking out on that field for the coin toss to face Ohio State and that it was my last game at Michigan Stadium."

That was the perfect way to cap a career. "What a humbling experience," Falk said. "What a great experience. Tom Brady was right. When

The marquee at The Big House honors Jon Falk during the final game of the regular season—against rival Ohio State—in 2013.

you're a captain of the Michigan football team, it's something you will never forget. It's an honor I'm confident that it will live with me for the rest of my life."

During the first timeout of the first quarter, Michigan lit up the gigantic scoreboards with tributes for Falk from coaches Hoke, Lloyd Carr, and Gary Moeller. It included highlights from Falk's career. "I thank Brandon and Hoke for treating me the way that they did during my final season," Falk said. "I thank everybody associated with Michigan and all the Michigan fans for all the nice friendships they have always shown me and especially during this bittersweet time."

Several times during the program, Falk had to fight the tears from flowing. "I was truly humbled by the entire program," Falk said. "I knew Cheri was up in the Al Glick Suite for the final tribute. I understand that Cheri and Nicki and Katie and Joe and every one of my family members were crying.

They all know how much the University of Michigan means to me, and I was saying good-bye."

Despite the loss, after the team got back to the locker room, the players lined up to shake hands and say good-bye. "Some were getting pictures with me," Falk said. "Several wanted me to meet their parents. The parents thanked me for the help I gave to their sons and wished me luck for the future. It was just something that you never even think about until it happens to you."

Chapter **27**
One More Time

So will there be another uninterrupted 40-year run at such a pivotal position as football equipment manager at a major college such as the University of Michigan?

Highly unlikely.

Can there be another such run that dares any candidate willing to accept an 80-hour week during the football season and a more normal 40-hour schedule during the offseason?

Probably not.

Can there be another Jon Falk?

Absolutely not.

Years from now—probably even decades—Falk's name will be remembered with a smile and the confidence that the old football equipment manager was truly one of a kind.

It's strange to view the sidelines on a football Saturday at The Big House and not be able to see the hulking figure of Jon Falk. But once in a while it's easy to hear Falk's hoots and hollers coming from one of those luxury suites where he has been invited to enjoy those games.

Perhaps the words of Bob Denari capture the essence of Jon Falk felt by each coach he has ever served. The two met in 1965 when Denari became the varsity basketball coach at Talawanda High School in Oxford, Ohio, from which Big Jon graduated before graduating from Miami of Ohio.

An entry written by Denari on October 17, 2010, says it all. It reads:

One of a Kind

Back in the summer of 1965, I was offered the job as head basketball coach at Talawanda High School in Oxford, Ohio. After signing the contract at Talawanda, I held a meeting for all boys interested in trying out for the team. It was a June evening at the high school, and I had concluded with all the information and excused the players. As I was about to leave, a young man approached me, stuck out his hand, and without hesitation said, "Hello Coach, I'm Jon Falk, your manager." At that moment little did I know that I had been greeted by the absolute model of what an athletic department manager would be.

During the next two years as coach of the Talawanda team, I never picked up a towel, cleaned a basketball, or hung up a uniform. These chores were carried on by Jon who maintained the equipment in what was known as the "athletic cage." On Saturdays Jon was in the cage by 8:00 AM and had the laundry done and uniforms distributed to the players' boxes.

On away game nights, Jon would have all of the equipment ready for the bus trip and unpacked when we arrived in the opponent's gym. Two younger students worked as managers under Jon's supervision. During home games, Jon made sure all of the needs of the coaches were met and that the scorer's table was set up. Jon would meet coaches' wives and children and take care of their needs during the game.

Upon graduation, Jon enrolled at Miami University in Oxford where he worked as a student assistant to the athletic equipment manager. When Jon graduated from Miami, he was offered a full-time job with an emphasis on the area of football. Three years later Jon received a phone call from coach Bo Schembechler at the University of Michigan. The job of football equipment manager was offered. This would mean that Jon, with Miami red within his veins, would have to leave his beloved Oxford.

Jon moved to Ann Arbor in the summer of 1974 and has been a great part of Michigan football ever since. He has been part of 37 bowl trips with the Wolverines... not bad for the Talawanda manager.

Some of my many memories of Jon go back to our daily H-O-R-S-E game at lunch time in the Talawanda gym. We even drew some crowds, and Jon would love to, as he called it, 'swoosh' one in from 30 feet.

Yes, Jon Falk was and still is *One of a Kind*. Ask anyone from Oxford, Miami, or Michigan.

—Bob Denari

Epilogue: Helping Harbaugh

Shortly after Jim Harbaugh returned to the University of Michigan as the head football coach, he and Big Jon Falk huddled together for a few words about the team just as they did when Harbaugh was flinging footballs and directing a lethal running attack when Bo was the coach.

Falk loved watching Jim fire the football on a 40-yard route or keep the ball himself while shaking off frustrated would-be tacklers on 20-yard keepers. "He dared opponents to stop him any way they could," Falk said. "Whatever Michigan needed, that's what Jimmy would give us. I wish Bo would have seen Jim with the earphones on and running the game real similar to the way Bo did."

Falk is careful to caution fans not to expect too much the first couple of years. But he's confident that under Harbaugh, the rebound is on its way. When Falk was hired by Bo, now more than 40 years ago, the coach told the rookie it was Jon's job to do whatever he was asked to do to win Big Ten championships.

Now more than four decades later and officially retired, Falk still is called upon to lend a little help with some sort of assignment that would help Harbaugh or any person on the team. "You don't say no to any coach, staff member, or player on the team," Falk said. "You help get the situation settled. That's the Michigan way."

Inside the Numbers

Jon Falk's overall record at Michigan was 353–130–7 during a total of 490 games. From 1974 through 2013, Falk's record at The Big House was 212–47–3. On the road he was 141–83–4.

During his 40 years at Michigan, Big Jon was always busy around the New Year holiday. He was part of 37 bowl games, including 14 Rose Bowls. His bowl record is 16–21 includes the Rose Bowl (4–10), Gator Bowl (1–2), Outback Bowl (1–2), Citrus Bowl (2–1), Sugar Bowl (1–1), Holiday Bowl (1–1), Hall of Fame Bowl (2–0), Alamo Bowl (0–2), Orange Bowl (1–1) Bluebonnet Bowl (1–0), Fiesta Bowl (1–0), Capital One Bowl (1–0), and Buffalo Wild Wings Bowl (0–1).

Acknowledgments

Looking back over my career, I must say I would not have been able to achieve the success I did had it not been for my family and friends who have helped me throughout my life.

My mother would take me to grade school every day and wait for me after basketball practice to take me home. That's when I began my interest in athletics. I soon realized I was not a very good athlete, but I loved the team sports. I watched football, basketball, and baseball on television or in person.

When I went to Talawanda High School in 1963, I knew I could not play football, but I went over to watch the team practice. The football coach, Marvin Wilhelm, asked if I wanted to play. I said no, but I would like to help the team. He said, "Well, you could be the equipment manager." I asked what a manager does. He said whatever the football coach tells me to do. I could do that, so I began to learn what it took to be a team manager.

I became the equipment manager for coach Marvin Wilhelm and the basketball manager for Connie Inman, Gary Stewart, Bob Denari, and Clark Froning. I also was the baseball manager for Wilhelm and Bob Purcell. I learned from these men and the players how to win and how to work with the players and coaches.

Many people helped me through my years in high school. I grew up on a farm, and when it was time to graduate from high school, my mother wanted me to go to college. My dad, William Falk, wanted me to stay on the farm and help him. My mother won out, and I went to Miami University and lived at home.

In the summer of 1967, I went to the Miami athletic complex and was heading to see the trainer Jay Colville to see if I could help out in the training room. As I was walking past the equipment room, Watson Kruzeski, the equipment manager, saw me and asked if I was the manager in high school and then he asked me to work in the equipment room. I never made it to the training room. I worked for the football team, and the team was coached by Bo Schembechler.

Coach Schembechler taught me how to win and how tough you have to be to be successful. I worked for the basketball team under coaches Tates Locke and Darrell Hedric. I was the baseball team manager under Bud Middaugh all four years and earned four letters. During my sophomore year, the equipment manager, Watson, died before the season started. Miami had to play the University of the Pacific in San Francisco. Coach Schembechler called me to his office and said that I would be responsible for the equipment for the game.

Coach asked me if I had been to California before. I said no but that my dad had taken me to the Cincinnati stockyards quite a few times. Coach Schembechler laughed and said I would do fine in San Francisco. "Ol' Bo is gonna take you to California," he said.

After the 1968 season, Bo left and went to the University of Michigan. Coach Bill Mallory became the new football coach at Miami, and Bob Purcell, my old high school coach, was hired as the new equipment manager. As a student I began to learn how to get along with new bosses, which would help me in the years to come.

When I graduated from Miami in 1971, Dick Shrider hired me as the first full-time assistant equipment manager at Miami. I worked at Miami until February 11, 1974, when I became equipment manager at the University of Michigan. Schrider and Wayne Gibson, who was the assistant athletic director at Miami, taught me how to run the business end of athletics.

When I came to Michigan, I worked with Bob Hurst and Irv Arnold. I also had part-time help from Jim and Dennis Morgan. Herb Fredrick, who dated back to the Tom Harmon days, helped me polish football helmets for every game. For all of the assistants and volunteers over the four decades, I feel truly blessed. These include Ed Whited, Brian Hagens, Mark Payne, Ron Dunn, Danny Siermine, Denny Morgan, Lee Taggard, and John Daggett.

As the responsibilities began to grow, so did the position of full-time assistants. Bob Bland joined the staff in 1987 and worked football and basketball. Rick Brandt joined in 1997, and Brett McGiness joined in 2005. I thank all of these assistants for their service. I was able to hire student assistants who were called "Young Boys."

Former student assistants who are now full-time employees at Michigan are Andrew Roming, Alec Zimmerman, Nick Mancuso, and Bryce Pilz. Andrew, Alec, and Nick all work in the athletic department. Bryce works in the legal system at UM. Tom Lewand was also a student manager for me and is now president of the Detroit Lions. I also wish to thank Brad Berlin, who took my job as equipment manager when I retired.

Every equipment manager needs to have a great relationship with the athletic trainers. I was able to work with only five trainers in my career: Jay Colville and Ken Wolfert at Miami and Lindsay McLean, Russ Miller, and Paul Schmidt at University of Michigan.

I was proud to work for seven athletic directors at Michigan. They are Don Canham, Bo, Jack Weidenbach, Joe Roberson, Tom Goss, Bill Martin, and Dave Brandon. I also have a great relationship with Michigan's interim athletic director Jim Hackett.

I was fortunate to work for five football coaches: Bo, Gary Moeller,

Lloyd Carr, Rich Rodriguez, and Brady Hoke. I also want to thank Jim Harbaugh since he was named the new head coach. It meant a lot to me when he included my name along with Bo, Jack Harbaugh, Jerry Hanlon, Gary Moeller, Elliott Uzelac, Lloyd Carr, and Mary Passink at his press conference.

I also want to thank Bill Mallory, the former coach at Miami University, for whom I worked for five years. I was able to reunite with him and his family when his three boys came to play football at Michigan. I want to thank every football player and all athletes whom I have worked with through the years and also all of the top baseball coaches and managers and players I met through the years: Sparky Anderson, Johnny Bench, Tom Seaver, Pete Rose, Buddy Bell, Alan Trammell, Kirk Gibson, Jack Morris, Dan Petry, Dave Bergman, Jim Leyland, Clint Hurdle, and, of course, Barry Larkin.

The basketball coaches I have worked with are Johnny Orr, Bill Frieder, Tommy Amaker, and John Beilein. Baseball coaches are Moby Benedict, Bud Middaugh, Bill Freehan, Geoff Zahn, and Rich Maloney.

I am also proud to call Bobby Knight a good friend.

I am very proud of the fact that I was a founding father of the Athletic Equipment Manager Association. I was able to win the Equipment Manager of the Year in 2001 and was awarded the AEMA lifetime achievement award in 2008.

I want to thank Dan and Kathy Ewald for taking my stories and so eloquently putting them into words for the reader to enjoy.

The people I want to thank the most are my mother, Jean Falk; my father, William Falk; my grandmother, Rosella Land; my grandfather, John Land; my sister, Ann, and her husband, Mike Bell; and my uncle, Don Falk. Most of all I want to thank my wife, Cheri; and our kids, Joe Winkle, Nicki Pfefferle, and husband Kurt; Katie Falk; grandson, Joey Winkle; and granddaughter, Abby Pfefferle.

I want to thank Wes Lust and Extreme Dodge of Jackson, Michigan, for being part of the Michigan Athletic Department transportation teams.

Wes and his staff helped me in many ways. I would also like to thank Al Glick and his family and the Alro Steel Company for the kindness they have showed to me and the Michigan athletic department. Al lets me sit in his suite during the games, and it is a far different view from where I stood for 40 years.

Thanks for the support of so many good people such as Jim Schmakel; Bernie, Rick, and Mark Stone; and A. J. Pierzynski, and so many others.

Lou Piniella, who played and managed for teams, including the Chicago Cubs, Cincinnati Reds, and New York Yankees, said when he retired, "I've been in baseball for 40 years. I guess it's about time for me to get home and see how my wife and children are doing." That statement struck home with me. So after working 40 years for the University of Michigan, I too must get home and see how my wife and kids are doing.